ONE MORE TALE FOR THE ROAD

ONE MORE TALE FOR THE ROAD

THE NOVELISED ANTHOLOGY

CHUMA NWOKOLO

Lagos
2014

2003 edition: ISBN: 978-2190-04-7 by Villagerhouse.

This edition: ISBN: 978-978-2190-18-5
Other Books by Chuma Nwokolo, Jr.

African Tales at Jailpoint
Diaries of a Dead African
Memories of Stone
The Ghost of Sani Abacha
How to Spell Naija in 100 Short Stories
The Final Testament of a Minor God

Gwandustan Limited.
No 99 Ogunlana Drive,
Surulere, Lagos, Nigeria.
Email: info@gwandustan.com
www.gwandustan.com

Distribution:
SEVHAGE
S 23, Top Floor, No 62, Old Oturkpo Road,
Makurdi, Benue State

Dedication

for my children, Zitam, NkeA, Lota and Gozim,
whose refrain, *'one more tale for the night'*,
has stoked the spirit of the storyteller...

Chuma Nwokolo, Jr.
12th August, 2003

CONTENTS

THE GATHERING

Ψ

Ma'Kanu was dying, and the family was gathering.

It was a simple thing like this that proved beyond all doubt that Odozi, despite her famous convent, was really more village than town: Igwe Nza had ostracized Ma'Kanu some days earlier and his decree had fallen like an invisible chicken coop around the retired school-mistress' deserted home. Even the teenage housekeeper succumbed to the invidious blackmail and abandoned her half-earned salary. On Tuesday night however, the dying woman had a particularly bad fit of coughing, which pricked the conscience of her nearest neighbour, Dada. At the crack of dawn, while Odozi's snoops were still asleep, she slipped through Ma'Kanu's fabled flowerbeds with a bowl of honeyed pap.

Dada had taken one look at the lonely woman's cancer-ravaged body and bullied her ancient bicycle all the way up to the Postal Agency near Odozi Junction. She had roused the phlegmatic proprietor and telephoned the youngest daughter, Ezinne, a kindergarten teacher in Idah and the closest to Odozi. Ezinne literally dropped her chalk when the message came from the Teachers' Common Room. She spent another half-hour by the phone, anxiously sending word to the rest of the children. Kanu's elopement with his sister, Udeme, had opened a gulf in the family, but if the imminence of death didn't bridge it, nothing would. By 12 noon she was kneeling at the foot of Ma'Kanu's bed in Grace Lodge, the cabin that villagers derisively called Orphan House, massaging her troublesome ankle joints.

Ezinne was an earthy woman. Having no airs herself, she was gifted with an incredulous laughter that could strip conceit off the arrogant. She was most comfortable amongst unpretentious children; and in that sense, her foster-mother, Ma'Kanu, had never grown up. Yet, that afternoon, Ezinne was not feeling particularly comfortable as she massaged a knob of liniment into the gnarled, arthritic limbs. She knew it was the end of the road for the old woman, but the reality was still daunting and she could do nothing about the fright in her eyes. She had never seen her mother quite as gaunt. It's not that same... She swallowed. I thought the remission was...

Ma'Kanu's feeble laughter provoked a fit of coughing which quavered on, a small, backfiring generator. It was difficult, looking at her now, to see the irreverent little dynamo that had turned the rundown Community School into the institution of choice between Enugu and Makurdi. But it was not impossible. She had taken life in her stride; what had broken her was disillusionment: five years after her retirement, her patchwork family was back in pieces and her old school had reverted to the bottom of the league tables. With her life's work effaced, it was as though she had never existed.

The fruit is ripe. She managed eventually, wiping tears that were not quite from laughter and not really from pain. Once the fruit ripens, it falls.

When Tobe arrived from his fish farm in Oguta, Ezinne was in the kitchen boiling the cocoyams for the ede soup. He entered through the back door, ducking as he came through the doorway to dispense a hug to his sister and a large tilapia into the refrigerator. Tossing his bag into the old Boys' Room, he went in to greet Ma'Kanu. She was sleeping as he stood over her. He could feel the old floorboards creak as he rocked to and fro. He could perceive the familiar smell of pigeon droppings in the low ceiling. He was back home; but it was not the same. Ezinne was a good cook, but Ma'Kanu only had to spend half-an-hour in the kitchen to release an aroma that literally plucked visitors in from the street. As his huge hand settled apprehensively on her shoulder, her eyes trembled open.

How are you feeling? asked his fingers. Her own hands were too tired for speech, and she mouthed a reply, slowly. She was almost out-suffering Job, she explained, only half in jest. But thank God for her dreams! She dreamed a lot about children these days. Flowers and children. Only the night before she dreamt of her long dead orchid! She wished she were strong enough to sit on her veranda and drink in her flowers, and watch the kids at their water games at the public tap.

Generally speaking, it was a dangerous thing to make a wish in Tobe's presence. He was not a man of any words but his actions compensated for that deficit. He had spent his first twenty years with the intense squint of a man struggling not to miss a punchline. In his fourth decade he had grown a confidence that calmed that intensity, without diluting the powerful generosity of spirit that made him both unpredictably bighearted and dangerous when thwarted.

Right afterwards he strode down to Bacha Line near Odozi Market, where the mad cow had gored a woman fatally back in '86. He hired some tools with which he sawed and planed the timbers of a blind wall right down until a surprised new door gaped out of the left flank of Grace Lodge. One could then look from the living room, over Ma'Kanu's rich flowerbeds, running luxuriantly wild since the advent of her invalidity, right down to the public tap in front of Okolie's house.

Then, as curious village children observed his door from a distance, he went in and moved his foster mother tenderly onto a couch. He was sobered by her weight — or more accurately, the absence of it. Even as he carried her, she held on to a small bundle. It was wrapped up in a rich purple length of velvet with tasselled ends. He had scooped it up earlier along with the beddings but she had struck at him cantankerously. He had grinned and shaken his head at the eccentricities of age. Swiftly now, he broke down the ancient poster bed, reinstalling bed and occupant in the living room, and propping her up with pillows.

Within three hours she was able to watch the children and her flowers to her heart's satisfaction.

Further south, in Abonnema, the radio message had reached the base station after Somto had boarded the company speedboat for his one-month rotation on the oil rig. He had been hailed by megaphone and after debarking to receive the news from the Port Harcourt head office he had grimly pulled off his hard hat, stripped off his life jacket and removed his gear from the prow of the speedboat. My Ma is dying and I'm going to the village, he had told his supervisor, pulling a notepad from his gear.

His supervisor was a sixty-year-old, hard-boiled oilman from Houston. He had worked with Somto only six months but already he knew that the easy-going man that the work gang called 'the Saint' could always be relied upon to take instructions. Don't be a goose, he'd warned Somto, you're still on probation, miss this trip and you'll lose your job. — But don't worry about the old woman; I heard the same thing three times before mine finally kicked the bucket.

Somto had been surrounded by several other world-weary types, all clad like him, in orange overalls, as he ripped out his application for a casual leave and passed it on to the amazed officer. I didn't say *the old woman*, he had explained as he turned for his jeep in the car park. I said my Ma; and I'm going.

He hadn't hesitated over the decision, but that didn't make it any easier to reach: his heart was pounding for the first hour of the drive to Odozi. Over the last decade he had done a dozen jobs in as many towns. He had stalked this one, his best yet, for a year and a half before landing it six months earlier. Yet, if he met his foster mother alive, it would be well worth a sack.

That drive itself was his longest five hours yet. For perhaps the first time, his well-used cassette deck was silent throughout the trip: the hours were barely enough to wonder how nine months had slipped past since his last visit to Odozi. The family had been pulling apart since the nasty business between Kanu and Udeme. Of course the root of his own disillusionment stretched back to his adolescence. Denied any knowledge of his real parents, he had been gutted to discover that 'Wiggle' wasn't even the original surname of the secretive Ma'Kanu. Quietly, he had dropped the surname. When importuned for a last name, he'd chopped his first name, Somto-Chukwu, in two to satisfy protocol.

Yet, Ma'Kanu was dying. Surely, that changed everything.

His muffler was broken again. By 2.20 pm the familiar roar of his gray jeep descending the hill from the old convent brought a smile to Ma'Kanu's face, a good ten minutes before he clumped up the wooden steps of the veranda to hang his baseball cap behind the door in a twenty-year old gesture.

It was almost 4 pm before Agabi's interstate taxi, which did the Enugu-Odozi shuttle thrice daily, brought Njide into the village. She had arrived at the Enugu Motor Park from Obubra since 1 pm. After a nail-biting wait for passengers to fill the cab, she had paid for all the seats and they'd set off on the fifty-minute run into Odozi. As Agabi pulled to a halt in the Odozi Park, she forgot her bag in the taxi and ran all the way to Grace Lodge, barely acknowledging the greetings of the bemused Acha sisters frying gari a little before the public tap.

Yet, when Njide finally reached the side-gate into Grace Lodge, she couldn't go in. All their lives, Ma'Kanu had been quite emphatic: there were to be no tears at her deathbed; there was to be no weeping at her funeral. Gripping the bamboo palings fiercely, she stared at her shoes for a long minute as she caught her breath, thinking desperately of her graduation, and when that failed, of her wedding day — which was a big mistake.

She wasn't to know that the family was at that moment watching her through the trembling muslin of Tobe's new living-room entrance. When the tears were in full flood she hissed with feeling and turning from the gate, hurried further down the lane to the refuge of Ekwutosia's provision store.

There was a long silence in the living room, then Tobe returned to the corner of the room. He knelt in the fine sawdust on the floor as he resumed the painstaking planing of the door panel with which he would seal the new entrance by nightfall. Somto was at the foot of Ma'Kanu's bed, plying her swollen joints with an analgesic liniment.

This crybaby of mine! Fretted Ma'Kanu, as a grumbling Agabi stomped up the veranda with Njide's forgotten travelling bag. She must be crying her eyes out somewhere!

Ezinne was sitting by Ma'Kanu's head, soaking and wringing out a face towel, which she laid, from time to time, on the old woman's feverish forehead. Let me check the soup on the fire, she said, escaping into the kitchen before her own tears came.

No one contradicted Ma'Kanu.

An hour afterwards, Njide finally entered Grace Lodge. The rest of the children had grown inwards, but she had flowered outwards, accumulating far more cares in her tumultuous marriage than her constitution could bear. It had slurred her physical beauty, with her accumulating a kilogramme or two for every year over thirty. Her face was careworn, her eyes, darting with an anxiety that, though currently focused on the woman on the bed, was plainly part of her lifestyle. She had a wan smile in place and an unaccustomed pair of brown glasses on her nose bridge. She hugged her brothers and sister quickly, and wordlessly embraced her mother. The heat from Ma'Kanu's corrugated cheeks alarmed her. Dropping her handbag, she took the towel from Ezinne, but within a few minutes, she was sniffling and her sister pushed her gently from the bedside.

Njide busied herself in Ma'Kanu's room. Tobe's evacuation of the matriarch's bed had exposed a confusion of cartons and boxes under thick coats of dust. Odds and ends, accumulated over the decades, had taken refuge under the bed. She fell to sorting and cleaning, glad for anything to take her mind away from the sombre reason for their presence in Odozi.

Somto had taken down the thin drapes in the four-room cabin and carried them down to the public tap to wash. As he worked, an unconscious song had slipped from him, floating three hundred metres to bring an incredible scent of normalcy into the rectitude of the living room. Already the drapes were sunning on the clothes-line and the bamboo palings of the fence, while a balmy breeze aired out the mustiness of Grace Lodge.

Ma'Kanu lay trembling on her bed, slipping in and out of a restless sleep, savouring the long-forgotten sights and sounds of a gathering of the family.

With the coming of dusk, they ate together as they last did, per-haps a decade earlier; except that this time Ezinne took her own meal in between feeding Ma'Kanu. The food was the main course and the accompanying conversation was made halting by the pres-ence of a courteous death in their midst.

Tell us about Margarita, asked Ezinne, without much expec-tation. All Ma'Kanu had ever revealed about her family could be related in a sentence: her mother's name was Margarita and her brothers had died in a fire. She had arrived in Odozi just before Kanu was born. Her life before that was a complete mystery.

The old woman shook her head firmly. The past is dead.

Did she teach you how to cook? asked Somto, nonetheless.

How many brothers did you have? asked Tobe. Did you name us after them?

Where is your *real* hometown? asked Njide.

Their persistent questions brought a mood of thoughtfulness over her. Her eyes slid shut and they leaned forward expectantly, then she opened her eyes and nodded at Ezinne, Can I have some more soup? It's really nice.

Njide uncasked nostalgia by producing the cache of black-and-white pictures she had discovered while cleaning Ma'Kanu's room. A picture of a ten-year old Somto, in the self-possessed pose that helped to earn him the nickname 'the Saint', sent Njide into stitches — until they discovered one of her in her birthday suit at four years. The pictures passed from hand to hand, evoking sighs and laugh-ter, the old years flickering to life again in those precious moments.

Ma'Kanu shared silently in the mirth — until Ezinne put a pic-ture in her hand, a group photograph of Kanu, Ezinne and Udeme, with the exclamation: How we've grown! They continued to eat and reminisce casually, the pictures passing from hand to hand, but all the while they watched their foster mother discreetly. When the photograph was quietly ripped into pieces there was a collective sigh from her children.

A moody silence followed as a tremor of pain ran through the old woman's body. When it subsided, she breathed, Reminds me of the trick you played on me when Chekwa was born, she said. Whose bright idea was that one?

No one spoke till the culprit owned up. Njide hung her head and sat back against Somto's huge *ekwe* drum. Mine, Ma. I knew you were really mad at Kanu and Udeme, but I thought your love for children was stronger than any anger. I thought, if I could just get you to carry Chekwa for one day, your heart would melt towards his parents.

There was a faraway look in Ma'Kanu's eyes and a tension in the air around her bedside. It was the first time in thirteen years that the subject of Kanu and Udeme was being *discussed*; and in such quiet tones!

The child was beautiful, she mused, if I knew Udeme was already pregnant when they eloped, I'd have been suspicious; but it was just five months since they got married. When Dada brought what she said was a foundling to me, all I thought was: I was too old to raise another baby. Yet, she said she had sent to the Ministry in Enugu, that it was just for a week or so...

She turned her face fretfully and Tobe carried his plate around the bed to continue reading her lips. A pillow blocked his view and Ezinne began to amplify Ma's words with her hands, finger-spelling Chekwa's name: a week passed and I fell in love with the kid. I called him Chekwa. I decided he wasn't going to be raised in any orphanage... then you all started to drop in on those silly excuses. With those innocent looks in your faces. — And I *knew*. So I put down the baby. And I never picked him up again.

Why? Agonized Ezinne softly. Dada told us that the bonding was complete. You loved Chekwa, he cried all night for you to carry him again. Kanu is your only blood son. Chekwa was your only blood grandchild. He was your blood in a way none of us can ever be.

Ma'Kanu coughed painfully until Tobe brought a glass of water to her lips. His hand was trembling uncharacteristically. At length she replied, gaining strength from a vein of bitterness that seemed to physically overcome her features. I just grew cold inside. I couldn't bring myself even to look at the boy again.

Do you know, said Somto eventually, Kanu and Udeme stayed two days with Dada, hoping we could talk you around. They couldn't stay away from their horticulture business too long. Then they took their baby and left. Do you know that Chekwa sickened and died the month afterwards? Dysentery, they said it was, and Udeme has never taken in again?

She's more like you than any of us, whispered Njide, she's fostering *five* children!

They thought they saw a shadow flit across Ma'Kanu's face, but her shoulders only moved stubbornly. That's got nothing to do with me.

Several minutes passed. Tobe's big hands clapped, and when Ma'Kanu raised her eyes to him, his hands signed gravely over his food, It's been thirteen years Ma, forgive them now.

Ma'Kanu struggled to her elbow before anyone could come to her assistance. Her suddenly cold eyes locked with Tobe's. As long as I live, she said vehemently, never!

Njide swallowed and passed a swift hand across her cheek.

Ma, began Ezinne intensely, Did you ever *think* this thing through? It *wasn't* incest, only Kanu was your blood. You never formally adopted the rest of us. They should have respected your wishes, but it was *not* incest. It is *not* unforgivable.

The sexagenarian fell back on the bed, drained by her emotions. She pursed her lips, struggling to invest her remaining words with the depth of her feeling: It *was* incest, Ezinneamaka. They crossed a forbidden line.

Ma'Kanu shut her eyes. A few moments passed before she continued: How old was Udeme when she was kidnapped? Wasn't she four when ritual killers shaved her head? Weren't they about to butcher her when the woodsmen heard her cries? After her killers were lynched, didn't she sleep three nights at the Odozi Police Post? Did they find her parents? Did *she* have a clue whom her parents were? Where they lived? Did I need a court order to raise her as my own daughter? When she thinks 'mother' does she have another picture in her head? — If I raised you all and you don't have the same blood in your veins, then my life has been a waste. Let me die in peace, Ezinneamaka! Don't mention those names in my ears again!

Somto pushed his plate away as he lost the rest of his appetite. The same bitterness that kept him away from Grace Lodge was building again. An errant breeze lifted the thin muslin and a stray cat, stalking across the wide veranda, stopped in front of the new doorway. For a long minute, it stared at the grim Tobe rocking on his feet, then it turned and padded away, tail arched in a question mark. Somto looked from Tobe to his sisters, and found himself unable to flaw one half of his mother's argument: *they truly were one blood.*

Intuitively, he could *feel* the passion swamping the control of the silent giant as Tobe clapped his hands explosively and turned, striding away from his unfinished meal. His leather boots creaked angrily as he entered the kitchen and there was a violent snarl of metal as he drew an axe from the trunk of garden implements. In apprehensive silence they watched Tobe storm through the house, dropping over the steps from veranda to lawn.

On the bed, Ma'Kanu shut her eyes. Her children could tell she was not asleep from the twitching muscles of her eyelids. They could also tell she wanted to be alone. One by one they left her side. Unforgiveness was the other half of the argument and Somto would never accept that. He drifted out onto the broad veranda that ran right around Grace Lodge, trying to fill the emptiness ballooning inside him.

A stiff breeze agitated the heavy boughs of the *ube* tree. The knobby digits of its lower branches scratched the cabin's corrugated roof, whose rusty zinc sighed contentedly, like any grateful spouse.

It was building up to a cool night.

Somto descended numbly onto the lawn, folding the drapes neatly into a clean pile on the veranda where a single bulb held the darkness at bay. The stars were out and Odozi was even quieter than he remembered. A few of the homes he'd driven past were empty shells. Few of his age lived full-time in the village any longer; mostly very old folk and very young children. The pupils Ma'Kanu had taught at the Community School had grown up and gone away. What people remained were emptying towards Ikpe Quarters, less than a kilometre distant, where a wake was about to begin.

Somto left the last drape, still slightly wet, billowing on the clothesline. Behind him, plates and cutlery chinked sullenly as Njide and Ezinne disposed of the remains of the ill-fated meal. As he turned from the bamboo fence, he recognised old Givemore hobbling by on his cane. In his sprightlier years, the septuagenarian had done all manner of unpaid handiwork around Grace Lodge, provoking no end of gossip in Odozi. He was well-read and well-spoken but, perhaps because of the prison term in his mysterious past, he had only retired as a joiner from the local saw mill. A lengthy, village-style greeting ensued, giving Givemore an opportunity to catch his breath. His close friend, Chief Ude, was to be buried in the morning and his traditional wake would run from evening until dawn.

Between grief and arthritis, it would take the old man an hour to get to Ikpe Quarters. Somto climbed into his jeep and ran him to the scene of the wake, nodding his head all the way at the superlative blessings of an old man who had little else to give. These days, every time someone called him 'the Saint', Somto felt a fraud. His amiableness came to him like an instinct for which he could hardly claim responsibility, Besides there was a stronger instinct that he had practised all his life, an instinct like a steel trap-door, which he brought down on the swirling stew of wickedness inside him.

He remembered the terrible relief he'd felt after his wife, Getty, had died of a heart attack, setting him free to chuck the job and house his year-old marriage had chained him to. As he grew older he had drifted further from his dreams, the trap-door's springs had weakened, and his old nickname was becoming more and more irritating to his ears. When he returned, Ezinne was sitting alone on the veranda's topmost step, absently replaiting an unravelling braid in her hair.

Somto doused his headlamps, wondering as he did so, how his colleagues were faring on the rig. He had obviously lost that job. Again. He had known the pain of a difficult dilemma, and now, with Ma'Kanu's intransigence, was beginning to know regret as well. He killed the growl of his engine and negotiated the flapping curtain on the clothesline to join Ezinne on the step. He gestured at the living-room as he sat, but Ezinne only shrugged glumly. They were silent for a long while, lost in their private thoughts. He found some relief mixed into his regrets: six months on and off the rig, and he was already aching for a change...

In the silence they heard the dull crack of a broken tree from the direction of the lower valley. It was followed by a distant rustling, which ended in a thump muffled by the miles. They listened carefully; presently they heard the faint tap-tap of axe on wood as Tobe attacked another tree.

Njide tiptoed out onto the veranda, squeezing in between Somto and Ezinne. Somto dug a finger into her side. I don't remember *that*, he joked, but she refused to be drawn. She's really sleeping now, she sighed, folding away her sunglasses. She took a stick of chewing gum from Somto's shirt pocket and listlessly began to unwrap it.

Somto noticed the bruise on her temple and froze. He touched it softly, questioningly. Don't start that, Njide warned tightly.

I'll *kill* him, whispered Somto.

Njide laughed softly, in spite of herself. The Saint! she teased, for Somto had gone through childhood without indulging the fight phase. She looked at Ezinne speculatively, you know, maybe I should have driven Ma completely berserk and married Somto as well.

Ezinne smiled. You would have had to battle me for him!

Njide took Somto's trembling hand from her temple. She smiled resolutely. Somto, we're here for Ma, let's keep it that way, eh?

He looked away silently.

They watched Dada see off her bosom friend, Edna Okolie, for the last time that day. They walked side by side, deep in conversation, fifty-year-olds enacting a closeness rare beyond the teens. Usually one friend's attempt to see off the other resulted in another full-fledged visit — due to the proximity of their homes and the glut of gossip. Presently the villagers parted company by the public tap and Edna disappeared into her home. Dada turned briskly for home, slipping silently past the gate of Grace Lodge, her eyes trained on the ground.

That's strange, frowned a nonplussed Somto, Dada walked right past our gate without coming in!

Exactly, agreed Njide looking around, where's everybody? Where's the housekeeper we got for Ma? Ma'Kanu's dying and not a soul is here!

Ezinne sighed. Sad eh? Dada explained to me on the phone: Ma was in the Health Centre over the weekend with a high fever. Seems she got delirious and started babbling about how she burnt down the Afa shrine those ages ago!

So? demanded Somto nudging a toad off the bottom step with his boot. That's good for a laugh, after all these years.

It wasn't funny as it turned out. Turns out that Igwe Nza's piles were acting up again. He was in the ward across the hall from Ma.

Remember, it was the Afa oracle that broke the kingmakers' deadlock in his favour during the battle for his stool. Well, he discharged himself right away. One hour later his council had ostracized Ma.

Somto was incredulous. Thirty years of teaching their children, he marvelled, and they abandon Ma on her last night because of a wooden idol?

The villagers can stay home if they like, said Ezinne. I phoned New Bussa as well. Kanu was out of town and Udeme had to arrange for someone to run their business and care for their kids. But they'll be arriving later tonight. If only Ma will soften up, there'll be a crowd by her bedside tonight.

They fell silent as an ill-clad group of excited youngsters hurried past Grace Lodge, ushering a limping masquerade in the direction of Ikpe Quarters.

Of course, began Somto slowly, we could move her into hospital in Enugu this night...

Ezinne shook her head firmly. No. Her time has come. Better she dies in peace at home, than in a crummy hospital bed somewhere.

I won't call this 'dying in peace'! sighed Njide. Not with all the bitterness she's carrying to the grave!

Somto tossed his key-bunch at the moon and caught it as it fell back. What can we do? I hate to think I chucked my job just to come and see Ma off to hell! I wish I could go fell a tree.

They fell silent again, listening to the tap-tap of Tobe's anger, remembering how Ma'Kanu had taught him to work out his rage after he had nearly killed a young tormentor all those years ago.

I'd fell a tree myself if that would do any good, said Ezinne. Her voice was pained. How can the same woman be so loving and yet, so vindictive!

No one tried to answer that. Tobe's second tree fell. They listened for the tap-tap but it seemed his anger was burnt out. Tobe was more sad than angry that night. They still recalled the evening the Tansi kids had mocked him, mimicking his sign language by acting like demented kung-fu warriors.

He had not lifted a finger against them directly, taking out his fury instead on their family rubber plantation. All night long, Odozi had listened to Tobe's axe at work, but no one was bold enough to approach him and by dawn there were sixteen mature rubber trees that thenceforth only served for firewood.

Ma'Kanu had said nothing about which trees *not* to cut.

Half an hour passed before Njide rose. Give me a hand, Somto, she said, leading the way across the lawn into the outhouse where she had stored most of the stuff she evacuated from Ma'Kanu's room. They returned with two cartons, which they placed by the steps. As they straightened up, Tobe pushed the side-gate open and walked in trailing his axe. He slumped, breathing heavily, on the lowest step as Njide opened the cartons.

They watched as Njide produced, one after the other, the birthday, Christmas and other gifts they had made Ma'Kanu over the decades. Books, brooches, clocks, they were all there. Most of the gift-wrappings were still on. It was as though Ma had unwrapped the gifts only far enough to determine that she had no use for them, before consigning them into a basement of forgetfulness.

What's this? slurred Tobe's tired fingers.

Our toys; said Somto heavily, vocalizing and finger-speaking at the same time. We've been giving her what was convenient for us, not what she really wanted.

Exactly, Njide agreed, returning a parcel to the box to free her hands for speech. These are the baubles we used to salve our consciences over the decades. That's exactly what we are doing now. We are still self-focused! Here's a woman who made a lifetime commitment to us, not caring what it did to her future. We came in dirty, other people's problems; she took us in, no questions asked. Yet, when it came to the crux, did Kanu and Udeme consider her feelings when they eloped?

It was their life to live, said Ezinne quietly; it wasn't a loan from her. — Besides, it's been thirteen years.

Thirteen, stressed Tobe, violently.

It may have been thirteen years, insisted Njide, but what kind of years were they? Ezi, you live closest to Odozi, when last did you visit with Ma?

Ezinne hung her head. She ran two classes in her school. To make ends meet, she also gave private lessons for slower pupils up till 5 pm daily, including Saturdays. Nevertheless it seemed churlish, even to mention that now. Not this year, she admitted quietly.

I haven't come to see Ma in nine months, confessed Somto soberly.

And even then, continued Njide, when did you last strike up an *ekwe vesai* on your drum? You know how much she loves it. Somto stared at his fingers, as Njide smiled. Tobe's the best of us all. He is here almost every month with our allowance and the salary of Ma's housekeeper; and he comes with her favourite fish too. I haven't been home in six months — yes, I've got problems, but so does she! Now look at us, we hear she's dying and here we are! I'd say we're just doing this for our consciences — so that when she dies, we'll feel we've done our duty by her.

Ezinne stirred uneasily. You're coming down too hard, Njide, we love her...

Yes, agreed Njide. In our selfish sort of way. We fell out with her over Kanu and Udeme and withdrew into our separate lives. Perhaps if we showed just a little of the unconditional commitment — and love — she gave us, she won't be quite so bitter. Perhaps she might have something in reserve for Kanu and Udeme right now.

So what do we do now? Tobe asked, coming right to the point.

For a change, let's focus on her, replied Njide. Let's stop pressuring her for this or that and try and spoil her for a change. She paused for a long time. She doesn't have much time left.

Somto took a deep breath, unwilling to speak the despair that he knew was in all their hearts. He was like an evangelist summoned to pray an invalid back to health, whose first sight of the sick man swerved into a prayer for a swift and peaceful death.

The trouble with Njide was that the passion of her emotions went far beyond the bounds of the practical. There was silence as Somto, Tobe and Ezinne pondered what a woman on her deathbed could conceivably do with anything, but none of them had the courage to confront Njide with the thought. Near the tap, a toad emerged from a puddle and grumbled throatily.

*

What I really, *really* want? yawned Ma'Kanu. She looked around the four embarrassed faces around her bed. What sort of thing is this? An old woman is dying and you're asking what she really wants. What can I do with anything right now?

Therefore, Njide told her about the box of gifts she had discovered under the bed, their penitence and their resolve. As they stood there, four silent figures, it seemed to Somto that two decades had somehow slipped off them and into the drains and they were little delinquents once again, standing trial before the matriarch.

Ma'Kanu laughed, but her own embarrassment was plain. Maybe you misunderstood me. Maybe I was keeping them till I needed them.

And, maybe not, suggested Somto quietly.

She sighed. Her voice was very soft and Tobe leaned forward to lip-read accurately. Right now, what I need most is the salvation earned for me by my Lord Jesus on His cross. There was a long silence until she continued. And the next thing? I have it too, my children gathered around me as I go... she hesitated and corrected, eyes shifting guardedly, ... apart from the children I disowned, of course.

And the next thing? prompted Njide, leaning forward.

I... Ma'Kanu hesitated, what's the use!

Tobe clapped. What's the next thing Ma!

She inhaled deeply. I'd like you to keep my wake right now, she said dreamily. With me lying in state right here! A good, old-fashioned wake with proper songs and stories — not a single tear, mark you, — so by the time morning wakes, I'll be gone. Then you'll carry me off to my flowerbeds, no mortuary. Remember you promised that long ago: no crying for me, and no mortuary either. And don't forget: no villager should dig my grave, only my sons — that is, TobeOlisa and SomtoChukwu. Once I'm buried, you can cry all you want.

Ezinne was stunned. The eeriness that had floated around all evening settled in with a vengeance: the lying-in-state had commenced! What was a deathbed doing in a parlour otherwise? A wake with you still alive? she whispered incredulously. Why?

Because I enjoy stories, Silly, said the old woman with a flash of her old mercurial cantankerousness. She slipped her hand under her pillow, worked it into her purple bundle from which she drew a worn leather purse. She opened it and her story cards spilled out. She gathered and shuffled them with childlike excitement, not noticing the gloominess on the faces around her bed.

The prospect of a story-fest seemed to buoy her spirits, administering an analgesic that lifted her, for the moment, out of her pain. And why should the celebrant herself miss the party? she demanded, as she dealt one card each to every one in the room. She placed one in front of herself and paused: Should we really make it interesting? Two cards each?

There were four shakes of the head and she stowed away the rest of the cards with some regret. Her voice became dreamy: Of all those things I miss about my youth, most of all I miss those wakes of very old people, where there was death but not tragedy...

You're not *very* old, corrected Tobe.

I'm as old as I want to be, scolded Ma'Kanu. Then she continued in the same dreamy voice, We'd gather, after all the singing and dancing was done, we'd all gather in discreet circles around the best storytellers. We'd listen to story after story... The best wakes were those attended by in-laws from far away when we had a good chance of hearing new stories... I remember dreading the sunrise! She picked up her card and turned it face up dramatically. It bore a single word. Marriage! she cried.

No one else touched his or her card.

You're serious about this, Ma? Somto asked carefully. It was hardly credible that in nine months Ma'Kanu's mental faculties would deteriorate so rapidly as to bring her to a second childhood where she begged for a tale before bedtime.

Ma'Kanu's face became bleak. *You* were never serious about your question then. She sighed as they took up their cards reluctantly. Nobody revealed his or her own card and Ma'Kanu broke the strained silence with forced brightness. The next thing is flowers. I want to sleep under the pink roses. I have a young bed near the gates. You mustn't dig an inch wider than you need; and once I'm in, replant my flowers. I don't want a casket, just a blanket and this dress I'm wearing. I can't be so dead I won't smell the fragrance of my blossoms on my way to paradise.

The lightness passed and her breathing became laboured. Gripping a handful of bedclothes, she began to cough, the knotted veins standing out from her emaciated neck.

Njide and Ezinne lifted her to an upright position until she was able to expectorate, and massaged her chest until her breathing grew regular again. From her house across the fence, they heard Dada call: *Sorryooo!*

Coward! muttered Njide as they laid Ma'Kanu back on the bed. When she tried to rise, Ma'Kanu's thin fingers were like a vice on her arm. There's something else, she said, embarrassment written all over her, My bundle, I want it in my grave. — And, she said severely, you must promise not to peek.

Not to peek? laughed Njide, But you'd be dead! What does it matter?

Promise!

They humoured her, and turned down the lights in the room to help her sleep.

They spilled out onto the veranda again. In the gloom, Somto and Ezinne quietly rehung most of the drapes in the house while Tobe and Njide held a silent, intense conversation. A dark cat made Njide jump as it streaked along the veranda. It went up the trunk of the *ube* tree on the heels of a fleet quarry. From the darkness of the thick foliage above, a rat squealed once and fell silent.

As Somto and Ezinne returned to the veranda, Njide's hands were moving jerkily as she lamented. I've goofed, now I've gone and raised her hopes for nothing!

What do you mean for nothing? asked Ezinne, sitting down. She passed her card around. It bore the single word, Madness. There were a hundred different words on Ma'Kanu's ancient story cards and any five cards could come together to task a skilled storyteller into a unique tale on the fly.

Njide looked at her appraisingly. Have you had time — in the last ten years to sit in on a moonlight session? When was the last time you actually told a tale?

This afternoon. Ezinne replied sprightly, her blue fingernails catching the light. I told one of Ma's stories in my taxi from Idah. My travelling companions asked what I'd remember her for when she passed on.

And?

I told them *Inua and the In-laws*. Go on, show me your card.

You still remember *Inua*? There was awe, and a little bit of worry in Njide's eyes as she brought out her card. It held the single word, Love.

Marriage, madness and love, mused Ezinne, that's easy enough to combine.

Ma shouldn't have brought out the story cards. Complained Njide nervously. She expects to hear some new stories tonight. I don't know if I can still do the story cards.

The sense of the words hit Tobe with the rumble of a relentless tragedy. The storyteller wanted a story! His own card bore the word *Rivalry* in Ma'Kanu's handwriting, scrawled in a firmness that dated back to her earlier years as the fearsome headmistress of Odozi's community school. Rivalry. He turned the word around in his mind and the card in his hands. As if it were yesterday, he remembered walking home with Ma'Kanu one night after the President's assassination. The bus from Enugu had broken down several times and

Ma'Kanu, who was fetching him home from boarding school, was an hour afoul of the curfew when they ran into a knot of red-eyed soldiers at the Odozi Junction. The soldiers had already detained a dozen other villagers, but one of them recognized Ma'Kanu and called out: "It's the Storyteller, it's the Storyteller!" And they walked proudly home... Tobe breathed and declared, using his story card to declare in grand gestures that only a man with his height and heart was capable of: For Ma, I'll tell a new tale tonight.

Somto was silent, and trepidant. For Tobe had never told *any* story before.

He began to reminisce through three decades, recalling the magical nights spent on that very veranda, when Ma'Kanu would draw up her cane chair and weave worlds into existence with her voice and her fingers and the expressions of her face, infecting them — and not just them, but the children of the neighbourhood who gathered for the nightly treat — with her love of lore.

Go on, demanded Ezinne, give me your card. Somto. She took the card and groaned. Tortoise! she said, passing it around. I *hate* animal stories.

That's what I hate about story cards, said Njide nervously, there's always that one ingredient that spoils the soup!

There was tense silence in the yard. Ezinne began to mutter, Marriage, madness and love, rivalry and tortoise. Marriage, madness and love, rivalry and *tortoise*.

Shut up, groaned Somto, you're driving me mad! The memories began to flow, breaking through the discouragement that was silting up his love for Ma'Kanu. He remembered the Ebola fever outbreak at the end of a state-organised students excursion into a wild game reserve. Four of the twenty-four children on the excursion had already died before the Hospital Extension Team from Enugu came for Somto. The Health Officer was a demi-god in those days. Quarantine! he had screamed. Odozi may have been located in the lower ranges of Milken Hill, but the sixty-seven kilometres that separated the village from Enugu may as well have been sixty-seven years into the past. There were no facilities to treat anything as virulent as Ebola. It was either the Otawon Infectious Diseases Hospital or nothing.

Ma'Kanu visited Otawon, a desolate place. She found that the IDH was run in the interests of the outside society, rather than the inmates, who often came in with one and were buried with a cocktail of infections. A referral there was a deferred death sentence.

She took his antibiotic placebos and went AWOL, returning to Odozi and moving the other children to Dada's. She lived alone with the dying Somto until she nursed him back to health, to the grudging admiration of a stymied Health Officer.

Somto had retold his favourite Tortoise tale over and over: the fabled Tortoise had embarked on the new career of booty-hunter. He accosted the felon, Hyena, on a lonely country road and challenged him to a duel. Predictably, hostilities began to turn out against Tortoise who called a truce, offering to reprieve Hyena — on condition that the outlaw never mentioned the battle to anyone.

Ma'Kanu battled the haemorrhagic fever into remission. And her faith was too strong even for the mildest muscle cramp to afflict her.

Slowly he pledged, goose bumps breaking out over him: For Ma, I'll tell my best tale tonight.

She said no tears, sniffled Njide. All the stories in my head are already beginning to make me cry. And these story cards... it's been so long... I'll just stand there with five crazy words in my head instead of a story.

Three gunshots went off just then from the direction of Ikpe Quarters. Disembodied voices bore snatches of a boisterous dirge over the trees and shrubs that littered the tumbling terrain of Odozi. They could almost hear the stomping of children fleeing grotesque raffia masquerades. There would be more gunshots before dawn, for Chief Ude was a respectably aged man.

Ma would have a quieter wake.

Ezinne's eyes were shining, as they had shone that evening, ages ago, when Ma'Kanu had returned from the Nkiti Women's Procession where she'd lost her voice. The children had gathered and the Storyteller was hoarse! It was the first time anyone would stand in for Ma'Kanu on the evening veranda and she had fingered her youngest child for the honour, a thirteen-year-old Ezinne!

How Ezinne remembered being thirteen! She had walked in from school, weeping again: Is it really true that Ukata was my father?

Yes, Ma'Kanu had replied and let her cry.

Ezinne was no foundling. The ruins of Ukata's house were not quite three kilometres from Grace Lodge. Not only had he been an armed robber, he had been a mean-spirited cad as well. He had married Ezinne's mother, an innocent teenager who thought her new husband a promising businessman, on a 'business' trip to Auchi. Soon after their first child, Ezinne, was weaned, he successfully waylaid a Railways pay-van on one of the notorious hairpin bends on Milken Hill.

It turned out to be Ukata's last job, for the van was followed by a truckload of bored soldiers on the way to some mountain exercises. Yet, the thought of leaving his beautiful young bride to the arms of another drove the highwayman to the very depths of iniquity. He wrote a confessional incriminating his innocent wife with the most heinous crimes of his career. They were both shot at the stake well before Ezinne's first birthday. Ma'Kanu had rescued their baby from the lynch mob that went to torch Ukata's house.

The cruel children at school never let her forget it.

Ma'Kanu helped her discover that even if Ukata was her father, she could be something other than 'The Highwayman's Daughter'. Even then Ma'Kanu was Head Mistress of the community school. It would have been easy for her to cane the tormentors into silence — at least in Ezinne's presence. She chose instead to help the thirteen-year-old earn her own identity. It started that night when the village children gathered at the feet of the Storyteller, and she chose none else but The Highwayman's Daughter to fill her place.

Ezinne discovered herself that night, two decades ago, in the transfixed faces of children who had called her names earlier in the day. She discovered herself in Ma'Kanu's approving face, which seemed to swell with pride as her story progressed. She discovered her gifting in a passion that led her into training for a career in kindergarten classrooms. For years, she had been the logical choice for her school's Weekly Assembly story circles. She knew she owed a debt of gratitude to a woman who had turned her from a child of sorrow into a child of joy.

Tortoise and love, madness and rivalry, marriage... repeated Ezinne,... the longer you play with them, the more they become gossips rather than crazy words. Gossips that open up a tale. You pick your characters and conflicts, your settings even. You tap the shoulder of the first word and just listen... Soon you're listening to five garrulous gossips and all you're doing is turning down this flow and turning up that one. She paused, then she rose hesitantly and dusted off her skirt, Let's go inside. Ma's wake can now begin; I think I have my story.

THE HEALING OF REKIA

Ψ

'Madness has finally gone nuts!' declared Godiva the agricultural extension officer when she heard the news. 'How can it strike the most beautiful girl in Suleika?'

'And just one week before her wedding too!' swore the farmer who brought the gossip as she signed for her supply of fertilizer. 'God saved that lustful suitor of hers.'

'And punished that greedy father of hers!' agreed Godiva vengefully, as she closed her shop to go see for herself.

*

Rekia's father had not opened his own shop since the calamity. The parlour of his rented bungalow beside Lantan Bridge was full of long-faced sympathizers who filled every space on the red oriental rugs. Tiamiyu ran the oldest chemist in Suleika Township. He was popular on account of his penchant for holding celebrations at the slightest provocation. Because of that same policy, the house he had started in Suleika G.R.A. more than nine years previously was still stuck at lintel level, its unplastered walls mouldy with age.

The Chief of Suleika arrived on a condolence visit at the head of his palace corps. He had barely settled down on his regal cushions when Rekia began to laugh again.

Although they had bundled her into the innermost room in the compound, so penetrating was her insane laughter that the Chief's courtiers on the street heard it and shook their heads sorrowfully. In Binta's room, Godiva and the women comforting Rekia's mother broke into tears again, drowning the weeping of the grieving mother.

'How did it all begin?' inquired the Chief gravely, a wary eye trained on the entrance into the courtyard from whence the insane laughter issued.

'Wasn't it that very day you turbaned Taofik?' sighed Tiamiyu. 'Rekia was fine when Binta and I left for the durbar at your palace; she was pounding spices in the yard. When we came back it was a different thing entirely. She was wearing her matriculation gown...' He was silent for a long time, then he ended plaintively, his voice near cracking, 'and she was chasing chickens on the street with a pestle.'

'And such a beautiful girl too,' murmured the Chief eventually. 'Kai, this is really a terrible thing.' His emotional judgment was echoed with feeling by the other sympathizers on the rugs.

Inside her room, Binta was weeping, asking Godiva in a ringing voice that sent chills down the spine of every listener, 'Why? Why didn't I die in last year's cholera? Why did I survive to see my own ears with my own naked eyes?'

In the main living-room, the Chief took a deep breath and picked up the richly embroidered cap someone had forgotten on the rug before him. 'I think,' he said, caressing the cap delicately, 'that before the news spreads further, you should call in Maidokinta. They say he has a psychic technique.'

'He was here yesterday,' replied Tiamiyu with another sigh. 'It seems that his medicine made Rekia ... really angry.'

'Yes,' agreed Mehuti, who sat with his silent banjo on the rug across from the Chief, 'most of Maidokinta's medicine ended up on his face.' Mehuti was chief musician at Tiamiyu's perpetual celebrations. He was equally at home at utter tragedies as well, for his dirges were first-rate stuff. A calamitous strike of insanity was however a halfway house that left him stumped. All the same, he had hung around just in case; since the crisis started he'd eaten all his meals at Tiamiyu's house and had witnessed the humbling of the healer the day before.

The Chief interrupted his admiration of the rich, intricate needle-work on the cap. 'But they say he has a red velvet cape. They say once he throws it on a violent lunatic, let him be man or woman, giant or midget, he must fall down. He must sleep for three days and he must wake up sane.'

Tiamiyu sighed and gestured at the strips of shredded velveting by Mehuti's side, one of which he was using to beautify his banjo. 'Rekia ripped that famous cape to pieces yesterday. Maidokinta was carried out of here kicking and screaming like a lunatic himself. Chief, God will help me not to go mad in this thing.'

'ALL OF YOU WILL DIE!' screeched Rekia from the bowels of the house. 'ALL OF YOU WILL SURELY DIE!'

'That's true,' nodded Mamoud sagely. The bicycle repairer was rifling the deck of cards with which he supplemented his income at the gamblers' corner of Suleika Market. 'Notice how loonies say things that we're usually afraid to say. Eventually, all of us will surely die.'

'Is that how to comfort Chemist?' scolded the Chief, glad for an issue on which he could be regally assertive, 'By telling him that his only daughter now tells the truth?' When Mamoud had bowed his head, suitably contrite, the Chief turned to Tiamiyu and whispered confidentially, 'There is someone else, — except that his charges are normally exorbitant...'

'Who is talking about money now?'

'And the distance...'

'Let the healer be in Timbuktu,' swore Tiamiyu. 'I will send for him this very night!'

The Chief nodded approvingly. 'Then send for Mansa.'

'Mansa's on his way,' chorused the attentive men on the rugs. The Chief blinked rapidly.

'Prince Toma recommended him two days ago,' explained Tiamiyu. 'Mansa is due here any moment now.'

'Prince Toma!' breathed the Chief in a sorrowful voice, although deep in the inner recesses of his heart, a strange elation moved in a secret dance of revenge. Within three days, Rekia's husband-to-be, Prince Toma, had been translated from 'most envied' to 'most pitied' man in all Suleika. Yet, the Chief could not find it within him, truly, to pity the prince, for even the Chief himself had been a Rekia suitor.

Which eligible man in Suleika had not dreamt of wedding Rekia?

In Suleika, a father's decisions on his daughter's nuptials still had the persuasive power of a court judgement and the Chief knew that he'd lost only to Prince Toma's superior ability to complete Tiamiyu's nine-year-old building project; but it didn't make him a better loser. Now his voice pulsed with a sympathy that didn't reach his heart as he asked the questions he'd been dying to ask all evening. 'Where's Prince Toma? How's he taking it?'

Tiamiyu shrugged with the air of a man who had rather more important concerns than Prince Toma's state of mind. 'He's fine. He'll be back soon. That's his cap you're holding.'

The Chief dropped the cap.

*

Presently, duty discharged, the Chief of Suleika rose to take his leave. His muscular courtiers fanned into a guard of honour and the entire gathering rose respectfully to see him off; but at the door, Rekia's younger brother upset protocol by barging in excitedly to announce the arrival of three camels at the head of the street. It was Mansa, his assistant, and the messenger sent to fetch him.

Tiamiyu dispatched another fleet messenger to fetch Prince Toma while Mansa and his assistant were given a princely feast in the kitchen. The Chief delayed his departure in the face of the momentous development. Prince Toma arrived breathlessly, even before Mansa finished refreshing himself.

The prince was a portly, clean-shaven and well-dressed man with a lisp. He could hardly be described as 'bald' since, just in time, he had opted to shave all his hair by choice. The year before, a precipitate divorce had put him back in the marriage market for the third time in twenty years; but it hadn't restored his youth, and he didn't look the typical bachelor. He was ushered into the parlour where he bowed fractionally to the Chief.

Prince Toma could not forget that eight years before, when Suleika's chieftaincy stool was filled, it was only one vote in the kingmakers' council that cost him the rooms at the palace. He squatted in the space created for him on the rug beside Tiamiyu and the Chief. Prince Toma reclaimed his forgotten cap, which he placed carefully before him.

'It's good you're here. Chief,' he said confidentially when he had settled down, 'Tiamiyu and I wish to bring a small disagreement for the wisdom of your counsel.' Despite the seriousness of his situation, he couldn't do anything about the stubborn sarcasm in his voice.

'After the healing of Rekia,' warned Tiamiyu.

Prince Toma pursed his lips and sighed heavily, like one who had much to say, but neither the proper audience nor occasion. At that moment, Mansa walked in, noisily sucking particles of food from his teeth.

Mansa was a short, gross man with a head that went like a shuttle as he walked. It gave him an uncanny resemblance to a fatted fowl. He also had a pugnacious stare and a truculently offensive manner; but such was the fame of the man that his minor eccentricities were easily forgiven him. He rejected the space offered him on the rug, preferring to pace the large parlour, stepping on the folds of many white caftans and speaking with a rather proprietary air.

'Show me a picture of this mad woman.'

'You mean my daughter,' said Tiamiyu, an edge in his voice.

'Is she not mad anymore? She may be your daughter or the daughter of the Queen of England, but she's mad and her madness is all that concerns me. '

Tiamiyu sulkily went to fetch a picture. While he was out, Mansa chuckled disagreeably. 'I like madness!' he declared with a glee that would have sat well on a wizard. 'People are so fake! When they have piles they clutch their stomachs... but with madness? Ha! There's no hiding madness!'

Tiamiyu appeared with a framed photograph showing a meltingly beautiful woman that brought deep sighs from many commiserators. Mansa refused to take the photograph. The healer stood, hands clasped behind his back, and made faces as he studied the picture, making of Tiamiyu a picture stand. He seemed to enter into a trance in the course of which his head shuttled faster than ever. He muttered a few incoherent sentences but, now and again, the Chief recognised the slurred word, 'beau...tiful'.

As suddenly as it had come on, he snapped out of the trance. 'It's a simple case,' he pronounced eventually, dismissing Tiamiyu and the picture by turning away. He curled his lips in disgust. 'If your messenger came with a picture, as I always tell my clients, I could simply have sent my assistant with a cure — and that would have saved you money too.' He snapped his fingers at his assistant. 'Fetch my bag.'

The healer's intimidating holdall, a blackened, ancient camelskin bag, was soon sitting in front of him. Every eye in the room was trained on Mansa whose gestures seemed to increase in grandeur and theatricality. Without even acknowledging the presence of the bag, he spoke again to Tiamiyu. 'I take my fees in advance.'

'Heal my daughter and you can name your price.'

'Whether or not I can heal a mad woman is not in question,' Mansa said arrogantly, 'but there's often a serious question as to whether or not my clients can afford my fees.'

Generally, Tiamiyu was a genial fellow. He chose an unfortunate occasion to take affront. 'How can you look at me,' he demanded with wounded dignity, 'the chemist of my community, in the presence of the cream of my society, in fact, in the very presence of my Chief himself, and suggest that I cannot afford your fees.' He lifted himself another inch above the short healer and thundered, 'Name your fees!'

The healer complied unemotionally. Then he added into the shocked silence that developed, 'I always take my fees in advance. From experience, I've found that the value of sanity tends to fall once a lunatic regains his senses.'

Tiamiyu's speechlessness was becoming embarrassing to the cream of his society. He fidgeted with the picture of his daughter as he considered how disgraceful it would be, in the circumstances of his boast, to attempt to negotiate the outrageous fees. Then he coughed, took Prince Toma into the only private enclosure left in the crowded house and shut the door behind them. Yet, such was the flimsiness of the toilet door —

and the emotion in their voices — that he needed not have bothered.

Their exchange was brief but heated and there was a moment of anxiety in the parlour until Prince Toma relented and started counting out currency notes in his stertorous voice. The Chief nodded approvingly as a shamefaced Tiamiyu stepped out of the toilet with a wad of currency in his hand. Mansa did not condescend to touch the money and it was counted into his assistant's hands.

'Take me to the mad woman,' he commanded when the transaction was satisfactorily concluded.

'My daughter is in a back room. There're some men with her to assist you. Only yesterday...'

'I always see my patients alone.'

'Is that advisable?'

Mansa snorted derisively but did not deign to reply. He was taken to the room in the back. The men who had been guarding Rekia were recalled into the parlour and Mansa entered the room alone, flourishing his charmed cowhide whip. He held a single vial of a dark concoction in his hand. His attendant, a lanky youth, deposited the camelskin bag by the door to Rekia's room and drifted back to lounge at the entrance to the parlour. There was a look of ineffable boredom on his face. Everyone else waited expectantly.

The news of Mansa's arrival had filtered into Binta's room and the red-eyed, matronly woman was led out by her friends. As she entered the presence of the Chief, she was demanding aggressively, heedless of protocol, 'He has come? The man who will heal my daughter, he has come?'

From right behind her, Mansa's assistant assured her rashly, 'Don't you worry, Madam, the mad woman will be healed within the hour, I have seen...'

The thickset Binta swung around and laid such a slap across his cheek that even the Chief winced in sympathy, 'You lunatic! How dare you call my daughter "mad woman"!' The assistant recoiled and slunk off to the backyard where he sulked by Rekia's door. It was right after that that the racket began. To the worried faces in the parlour, it seemed that all the furniture in the back room was being systematically trashed.

Expectedly they heard Rekia's screeches, which seemed to be escalating rather than subsiding. The Chief thought it fortunate that Binta had not seen Mansa enter her daughter's room alone, with the wicked-looking whip. Expectedly too they heard Mansa's voice, rather less arrogant than before; and it seemed to bleat, in rising alarm, right after every lash of the whip.

It did not sound as though there was an exorcism in progress.

Prince Toma had displayed a rising discomfiture with Binta's entrance into the parlour. Now, he folded his cap into his pocket and mopped his clean-shaven head on which large droplets of sweat had consolidated. Then, taking advantage of the racket that focused every attention in the living room on the happenings in the backyard, he rose casually to his feet. He then wandered towards the main entrance with the air of a man seeking a breeze.

It was no use. His sinuous movements caught Binta's eye and she snorted, in a disorienting leap from the depths of grief to the heights of fury. 'What are you doing here, you wizard? Shouldn't you be creeping around the local festivals laying your traps for another innocent girl?'

Prince Toma froze as though he had taken a friend's dagger in the back. He slowly raised his closed eyes to the ceiling with the air of the innocent crucified. Every eye shifted expectantly to this new and promising tableau. The Chief looked with wonder at Binta, whose voice he was doubtful if he had ever heard before that day. It was uncanny how one madness in the family quickly spread like wildfire.

'Chief!' shouted Binta, and the dignitary flinched. 'It is good that you're here! It's good that both the wizard and the judge are in the same room today...'

'After the healing of Rekia,' said Prince Toma tiredly, turning to the Chief for mercy, like a battered pugilist appealing for the bell, 'isn't that what her husband said just now?'

'"Whath her huthband thaid",' mimicked Binta furiously, 'he even talks like a snake! My daughter's first ailment and he flees! I should have listened when Rekia begged not to be married to a baldie older than her father! I should have listened when she said her true love was Enoch!'

'Quiet, Binta,' said the Chief in his calmest and most authoritative voice, and to his great relief, she fell silent. He turned to Prince Toma, affecting wonderment. 'What's this I am hearing Prince Toma? You want to break the betrothal? With the wedding only seven days away?'

'With the cards already printed and posted,' stressed Tiamiyu, an angry finger wagging at his prospective son-in-law.

'With my gift already purchased and parcelled,' added Godiva from Binta's side.

Prince Toma deliberately mopped his head and ears again before turning squarely to the Chief. He had the air of someone that, having gotten over his dismay at being pulled into the mud, had come to terms with his predicament and decided to deal with his tormentors. He said severely, 'I have told these people...'

'Aha,' interjected Binta, stretching out her arms to the Chief for mercy, as she maliciously exaggerated Prince Toma's lisp, 'his parents-in-law have become "dethe people".'

'I've told them,' said Prince Toma, trying to ignore the interruption and the insidious laughter, 'they can keep the gold necklaces and the plates and the clothes I bought for Rekia. They can keep the trunk box I gave her. They can keep the rice and the goats I brought for the wedding. They can keep the money I have paid on her head so far. They can even keep the blocks I've already moulded for their abandoned house...' He paused to allow the excited murmuring pulsing through the roomful of gossips to have its full course; then he ended resolutely: 'but they must also keep Rekia. Betrothal is not marriage.'

A hush descended over the parlour as Prince Toma sat down. Although a little gratified by the disclosure of his magnanimity to this ungrateful family, he was still deeply resentful at the public spectacle he had become. He had planned, first to postpone, then to quietly cancel the marriage. This public inquisition had no dignity at all.

'And if you see how he was dancing on the day of the betrothal,' murmured Godiva in a voice like an unseen reptile rustling in a bed of dry leaves.

'Everybody here was dancing on that day as well, as they ate my food,' said Prince Toma philosophically. 'But nobody is dancing today and I won't be the only person dancing. I am not a mad man. Betrothal is not marriage.'

'Look at him,' hissed Binta with overmastering disgust, '"wait another semester," I told him, "let Rekia finish her polytechnic course,". "No," he was begging me on his knees, "my love for your daughter is too hot!" Look at him now!' she hissed again, accompanied by every woman in the room and not a few men.

'If you were already married to her,' began the Chief tentatively.

'I didn't get to that bridge, Chief,' interrupted Prince Toma truculently. This was what came of picking a wife from an impoverished home; they were so desperate for a rich in-law that they'd balk at nothing to rope him in. 'I didn't get to that bridge at all. The egg has cracked in the hand of the seller. It is the seller's loss. If it broke in my hand, it would have been my loss.'

The Chief nodded and bowed his head as he reflected on a fitting ruling. It was at that moment that the silence from the backyard first seemed to dawn on everyone. 'He did it,' whispered Binta unbelievingly, 'he healed my daughter!' As everyone rose and surged for the door into the backyard, the main entrance door broke open again and Rekia's kid brother barged in.

'One camel is going!' he announced.

At the same time, Rekia's victorious laughter reverberated from the backyard. 'MY MONEY!' screamed Prince Toma so savagely that the Chief started to his knees.

'MY DAUGHTER!' screamed Binta in despair, then she began to wail, assisted lustily by her ululating companions.

'MY PEOPLE!' roared the Chief from his feet, but it was impossible to restore order until his people found Mansa's assistant skulking in the backyard with his master's bag slung on his shoulder and Prince Toma's money intact in his hand. He was ushered into the presence of the Chief with not a few cuffs. 'Where's your master the great Mansa,' asked the Chief with scathing sarcasm, 'the one about whose healing powers there is no question, the one who must see the beau...tiful woman of Suleika alone?'

'My master is a proud man. He climbed the courtyard wall; but he's not a thief.' The assistant offered the money to the Chief, but Prince Toma snatched it from his fingers.

'What about my daughter?' demanded Binta, blowing her nose.

'That is one very mad woman,' said the assistant, making his escape.

'YOU ARE ALL FOOLS!' screamed Rekia triumphantly from her incarceration; 'YOU ARE ALL BIIIIG FOOLS.'

'That's true again,' said Mamoud excitedly, before the Chief's withering gaze silenced him. The Chief panned his gaze around the room and when he had achieved pin-drop silence, he sat down regally and spoke.

'I have reached my decision. This is a sad matter, but there are sadder things that can happen to a woman which can still be solved by digging a grave.' He paused, struggling with himself as he tried to put aside his personal antipathy for Prince Toma in order to do his duty as Chief of all Suleika. 'On the question whether Prince Toma can dodge his obligation to this beautiful, young lady in the most distressing time of her life, I find that the elephant must first be shot before we can divide its meat.'

An 'Oh!' of disappointment rose from the womenfolk as the Chief pressed on, 'Yes, we can't decide who must marry Rekia till we decide who can heal her. For now, Rekia is... ill; and our tradition is that a father's doors are always open to his daughter, before or after marriage.'

'But a contract is a contract,' muttered Tiamiyu bitterly.

The Chief counselled. 'A vegetable seller whose wares are really fresh isn't desperate. For now, Prince Toma chooses to be seen as a family friend rather than a son-in-law. My judgment is, so be it.'

'Thank you,' murmured Prince Toma, looking smugly around at his persecutors.

'And when a family friend presses money into the hands of a man struggling to rescue his only daughter from madness, he doesn't look over his shoulders to see how that money is spent.' The Chief waited till Prince Toma had reluctantly separated Mansa's retainer from his billfold and passed it to Tiamiyu. Then he nodded at his courtiers and began to gather his robes, preparatory to rising.

'So what about my daughter!' Wailed Binta, setting off the womenfolk again, and the Chief lost all strength in his lower limbs. He sank back in despair, wondering how to escape this house of tragedy with dignity. He steeled himself and raised his voice above the clamour.

'There's also a place I know in Lokoja,' he began, forcing confidence and enthusiasm into his wilting voice, 'A psychiatric hos...'

'My daughter isn't mad' snapped Binta indignantly; 'I'm looking for someone to heal her, not an asylum to lock her into!'

The Chief pursed his lips silently. He knew that in the extremity of Binta's emotions it was easy even for a chief to get insulted. It was the chemist's duty to remove his wife discreetly from the parlour so that he could make his exit with dignity. He leaned over to Tiamiyu's ear.

That was the point at which Kisu rose gingerly and coughed to gain the attention of the packed parlour. 'I...I can heal Rekia.'

Mehuti risked the anger of the Chief with his laughter. Many others joined him, but the Chief did not take offence, chuckling as he was himself. It was a welcome relief to the high tension. Kisu was a twenty-five-year-old refrigeration technician in green overalls. He had finished his apprenticeship not quite eight months earlier. He had a small hunchback, which seemed to have grown bigger in the eyes of the villagers ever since a cruel friend had called him 'Tortoise' after a falling-out. The nickname had stuck. He was one of the most placid and harmless lads in the village; but nobody expected him to do much good either.

'Well, how will you heal her then,' asked the Chief good-naturedly, 'is it by magic or prayer? Is your style African or Chinese? Are you orthodox or naturopathic?... What is that in your pocket? Is that a stethosco...no! That is not a spanner in your pocket!'

'It'ssss a spanner,' admitted Kisu, twisting a button on his overalls in embarrassment.

'If Tortoise says he can heal my daughter,' said Binta impatiently, 'why are we still discussing it? Go ahead and heal her!'

'Or are you waiting for your fees as well?' asked Prince Toma with forced jocularity.

Kisu hesitated. '...Juuuust for us to agree the fee, Sir.'

The Chief exploded unexpectedly. It was a most peculiar thing, for he'd had no inkling that his top was in any danger until he had blown it completely. 'Didn't you see the great Mansa disgrace himself just now?' He demanded in a thunderous, unflattering rage that spattered his listeners with spittle. 'Okay, name your fee, I myself will pay it when the girl is healed, — but I will name my fee if you make a monkey out of me. If Rekia isn't healed, I'll give you one stroke of the horsewhip for every thumb and toe in your body! — And one extra one for that greedy hump on your back! NOW, NAME YOUR FEE!'

Kisu seemed momentarily nonplussed. He dropped uncertainly to his knees. He had never seen his sovereign so fulminant. The Chief, on his part, quickly regained composure, becoming deeply embarrassed by his incontinence. He could not believe he'd mentioned Tortoise's hump so unchivalrously. He'd never known madness to be contagious. Staunchly he resolved thenceforth to avoid theatres of insanity. 'What's your price?' He repeated quietly.

Kisu made two false starts before he was able to say, 'The haaaand of Rekia.'

The Chief's mouth dropped open.

'You will marry her?'

Kisu stammered hastily. It was clear that his garment was about to lose a button. 'Wwwwhen she is wwwwell, I want her hand. That is wwwwhat I mmmmean.'

The Chief stirred with some embarrassment. 'Actually, that's a price I can't pay myself. Tiamiyu,'

Tiamiyu smiled patronisingly. 'I think Tortoise will have to wait until...'

'You think nothing!' said Binta stridently, publicly contradicting her husband for the first time in her life. 'Right now the only consideration is my daughter, not bags of cement. There is nothing to think.'

'That is exactly what I was about to say,' agreed Tiamiyu lamely, amidst unfortunate laughter from people supposed to be condoling him. 'I think you should go ahead and heal her first... and then the marriage can come afterwards... and...'

'Follow him,' said the Chief to two well-muscled courtiers. 'If this particular healer escapes over a wall his reward will be multiplied on your backs.'

They escorted him to Rekia's door, pushed him in, and snatched the door shut behind him. One courtier took his place at the door, the other at the window near the wall. A chair was brought into the courtyard for the Chief and the apprehensive company waited for the bedlam to begin.

Tiamiyu's house was fuller than it had ever been before. Word had gone out about the strange happenings and the neighbourhood had emptied into the house, filling parlour, rooms, courtyard and corridors with whispered concern. Nevertheless, from Rekia's room, there was only a tense silence. Since her last opinion on the foolishness of the sane world there had been no sound from her.

'Perhaps she is sleeping,' speculated a worried Binta, 'perhaps she is unconscious, or wounded, perhaps that mad Mansa has even killed...'

'Nonsense,' said Mamoud with the air of an expert, 'lunatics don't die like that, haven't you seen them eating stuff from dustbins that would have killed us normal people?'

Binta's eyes flashed menacingly but the door to Rekia's room opened just then and Kisu looked out hesitantly, rather like the fabled tortoise fearing punishment for another bout of trickery, 'She's hungry,' he said, drawing his head back into his shell.

There was no reaction for several seconds then a phalanx of women stormed the kitchen, returning immediately with some plates on a tray. It was set before the door of the room. At the sound of the chinking plates, Kisu opened the door and carried the tray inside. Binta hugged herself wordlessly. Rekia had not eaten in the three days of her madness.

Nothing happened for ten minutes then the door opened again and Kisu looked out. His face was pinched and uncertain. 'Her cccclothes are torn, she wants some beautifuuuul dresses.' He drew in his head again, reappearing only when a knock on the door announced the clothes on the threshold. The curious courtier craned his neck but the door slammed in his face.

Soon afterwards the door opened and Kisu walked out quietly, shutting the door securely behind him. They waited for him to speak but he wandered through the milling crowd until someone made room for him on a wooden bench by the rear wall of the courtyard. 'So what about my daughter?' demanded Binta excitedly.

'She's fine,' replied Kisu vaguely, but no one made a move for Rekia's door.

'Is she healed?' demanded the Chief. 'Why are you sitting here with us?'

'She needs ssssome privacy,' explained Kisu.

'But is she healed?' insisted Tiamiyu.

'I... tttthink she seemed ccccalmer.'

'Did she eat?' asked the Chief suspiciously, 'Tortoise, is that oil on your shirt?'

He scraped at his shirt with a fingernail. 'This is... this is a ruuuust stain.'

'What medicine did you give her?' inquired Godiva superciliously.

'She sssssseemed to be nervous when I entered and I... I tttttalked to her...'

'Psychoanalysis,' muttered a heavily bearded neighbour, nodding knowledgeably.

'That's all?' asked Godiva insistently. 'You talked to her, and she listened to you and she asked for food?'

Kisu considered carefully, 'I sssssuggested some food, and ssssshe didn't refuse...'

'Then she asked you for clothes?' persisted the agricultural extension officer, who might have been an attorney. 'Did she actually ask you for clothes?'

Kisu shook his head slowly. 'I could see her cccclothes were torn and not ddddecent enough for a wwwwedding...'

'And she asked you for privacy? Is that why you came out?'

'...I ffffigured that...' Kisu's low voice tailed off.

There was a pregnant silence, into which Godiva snorted a private, derogatory opinion on cunning tortoises that tried to acquire wives without paying bride price. Binta began to wail again. The Chief issued orders and a group of four trepidant men approached Rekia's door, but when they tried it, it appeared firmly bolted from inside. One of the men put his ear against the door and his face grew puzzled. He hurried to the Chief's side and whispered to him. The dignitary frowned. 'Is there a shower inside that room?'

'Yes,' replied Tiamiyu.

'It seems that my servant heard a sound of bathing.'

Binta cleaned her tears hastily and went to listen, for her daughter had disdained her toilets since the day of Taofik's turbanning. Behind her, a long queue of people formed to listen at Rekia's door. Presently the listeners reported a humming — the sound of bathing and humming — which seemed a particularly sane combination of things to do. Soon there was silence. Then another excitable listener logged something that sounded suspiciously like the sigh any woman would heave when a hairstyle wasn't quite working out in a mirror; but it went uncorroborated and was discounted.

An hour passed. The pilgrimage to the door continued unabated. Some people had listened twice, others thrice. Only the Chief had refrained completely, it being beneath the dignity of monarchy to go listening at women's doors, sane or otherwise.

Occasionally the Chief was heard to mutter: 'If Tortoise is having me on...' When the last fifteen persons had reported a perfect silence from Rekia's room, a regal slipper began to tap restively. 'Shall we break the door?' demanded a solicitous courtier of his sovereign. The Chief hesitated and looked in Kisu's direction. The technician shook his head and swallowed.

'Maybe she's wwwwaiting for the wwwwedding music to begin.'

The Chief stared incredulously. 'Wedding music? She told you that?'

He shook his head '...I told her there'd be a wwwwedding, maybe she's wwwwaiting for the music of it...'

The Chief looked helplessly from Binta to Tiamiyu; but they avoided his glance. No one seemed anxious to take responsibility for authorizing what was developing into a major farce. Reluctantly, the Chief summoned Mehuti. In low tones, feeling that he was performing the most idiotic act in the eight years of his reign, he commanded the musician to play.

Well, Mehuti played. He was an icon at every celebration of worth in Suleika Township. He played for the rich and he played for the poor. His price was a meal and the notes pasted on his sweating forehead by appreciative celebrants egged on by his sonorous voice — which was simply made for praising.

However there was something wrong with his music that day. Normally he played with abandon, that day he played like a tap running to fill a cup. He played with his eye on the door to Rekia's room, which remained ominously shut.

Kisu lifted his hand hesitantly and the tortured melody from Mehuti's banjo trickled to an end. 'This doesn't... ssssound like a wedding... it doesn't ffffeel like a wedding. I think Rekia can reccccognise the sound of a wedding...'

The Chief stared at his elegant leather slippers for inspiration as Prince Toma cleared his throat significantly and said nothing. Belatedly, the Chief realised that madness had momentum. Just one foolish step and he'd found himself tumbling down a treacherous staircase of buffoonery. Passionately, he wished he had not waited for Mansa's healing. He cleared his throat interminably, but when he fell silent, he'd found nothing appropriate to say.

Gingerly, the crowd in the chemist's house began to produce other instruments of their own initiative. Flutes materialized from the pockets of several caftans. A conga was produced from the kitchen where its new goatskin was curing over the smoking range. The Damisas next door fetched a black agogo along with its stick. A brace of shekeres giggled in anticipation. Feeling slightly foolish, they cleared a space in the centre of the courtyard. Somebody produced the emblems of a traditional marriage: the wine and the glasses, and set them on a stool.

The Chief felt passionately that it was time for him to go, but his legs were heavy and immobile. He wasn't alone in the feeling. Mehuti was plucking tentatively at a banjo string when Kisu ventured, 'It seems she will pppprefer a ppppparticular song.'

'What's that?' demanded Tiamiyu sarcastically, convinced that the whole society had finally gone crazy. 'Here comes the bride?'

Kisu shook his head and coughed self-consciously, 'I'll sing it,' and he did. But when the musicians began to play, his less than robust voice was drowned, so that, purely as a social service, those who knew the chorus, or could learn it, picked it up and sang it.

The music had a logic of its own.

Binta started the clapping. When the Chief looked up with a start, her eyes were fastened on Rekia's door, as though she could sing and clap open the doors of madness. Moreover, when Binta glanced from the door to the womenfolk, her eyes appeared accusatory. It was as though their silent palms were a traitorous vote for the madness of her daughter. Therefore, one after the other, they began to vote for healing. The Chief was the last to join in; by which time the music was a reverberating celebration that was felt in the guts.

The door of Rekia's room took everyone by surprise when it opened and let her out. The first thing that struck them was the beauty of the woman. Mad or not, here was the most beautiful lady in Suleika. Then they noticed her shyness. Then they noticed the quiet. For the wedding music had tailed off into the astonishment of Rekia's sheer presence.

She slipped easily through the awestruck gathering. There were intakes of breath, and some inching for the doorways. She was shy. She looked, and turned away, eyes lowered and bashful. What was she seeking? Her limbs were lithe and graceful. Where was the strength and the fury that disgraced two healers and their artifices? Then there was the bodice and the head-tie, the hair that fell by arrangement from her netting. Not a wisp was out of place.

Where was the lunacy?

She passed the Chief; she dropped a curtsey; he checked his grin. Was there madness here or what? She passed the stool; she took a glass of wine. The crowd tensed. Was this a lucid interval? Would she presently make of the glass a missile? The silence was perfect but for those two hesitant heels clicking on the terrazzo of Tiamiyu's courtyard.

A tentative smile flickered for Mehuti, a wider one flared for Binta, whose arms opened; but Rekia turned away, urgently, eyes not so shy now, but searching boldly — and then! Stillness. Slowly, shy all over again, she followed her eyes and the crowd looked after her as she flowed towards Kisu, where he stood beside his best friend for many years who had dropped out of his apprenticeship programme to attend Polytechnic.

When she got there, she stopped, unable to lift her eyes, unable to look at him. Kisu smiled and everyone could read the devotion there. She stood, and slowly, beautifully, turned, seeking out her mother, then her father, with her eyes. The first movement of the crowd as they joined her, one on either side, in mute consent, as she consummated the traditional marriage by lifting the glass of wine to Enoch's lips to drink, Kisu smiling proudly on.

She started the song again.

> He has opened the gates of brass,
> And torn asunder the bars of iron.
> O, that men would praise the Lord,
> O, that men would praise the Lord!

That was when the wedding really got underway, as feet stomped and arms flailed, as though they would break open and tear asunder bronzen gates and iron bars. Of course, in the household of a man like Tiamiyu, especially when the stockpiling for Prince Toma's wedding had commenced, it wasn't difficult to quickly compound a feast of singular proportions.

Tiamiyu never had a better reason for celebration. Hours passed before the ecstatic crowd parted its sweating ranks to permit their Chief to depart. As he entered the cool night behind his train he paused and murmured in Tiamiyu's ears, 'This daughter of yours, this Rekia, what is she studying at Polytechnic?'

'Theatre Arts,' replied Tiamiyu, still flushed with relief at his dramatic deliverance from the jaws of tragedy. The Chief nodded broodingly. He was still nodding as he walked into the night.

Tiamiyu looked thoughtfully after his sovereign. Binta was pulling at her husband's elbow, anxious to return to her guests. 'God Almighty,' he whispered in a strangled voice, 'I think we've been had!'

'Yes, Dear,' she agreed absently, smiling pleasantly at the glowering Prince Toma, another hostage of the mischievous crowd, as he finally broke free and stalked home, capless once again. 'Let's rejoin the party.'

Ψ

Ma'Kanu was chuckling when Ezinne was done. Rascal, I know what you're selling, but I'm not buying!

Who me? Ezinne inquired innocently.

Yes, you! You had an extra card up your sleeve, but I can pick and choose.

It's got a marriage, signed Tobe, it's got rivalry,

Plus plenty of madness, agreed Somto.

And love, murmured Njide, a faraway look in her eyes.

The tortoise bit is tricky, apologised Ezinne.

Nonsense, Kisu was as cunning as any real tortoise, protested Ma'Kanu. She grinned again, Rascal, you, I know what you're selling, but I'm not buying! I saw where you were going halfway through!

That's because you're an old crook in the game, that's why!' laughed Ezinne.

Thanks anyway. Kneel, I want to bless you.

Ezinne knelt. She shook a pillow out of its case and draped the slip over her hair.

Somto gathered Ma'Kanu gently in his arms and raised her so that her skinny hands could rest on her foster daughter's head. Tobe dropped to a knee beside Ezinne, his eyes trained on Ma'Kanu's lips as she began to speak: I bless you with smiles, Ezinneamaka, I bless you with laughter. I bless you with goodness and I bless you with mercy — but most of all, my dear child, I bless you with the joy that flows from knowing God. The world may steal your sorrows, it will never find your joy. Your presence will bring peace, your speaking will bring light. Your life will justify the woman that bore you and compensate for the man that fathered you.

She paused for a long time, and when they glanced at her, they saw she was fighting to control her emotions Yet, when she eventually continued, her voice was as truculent as ever. Get up now, Ezinneamaka, before you take all my blessings.

She was panting as Somto gently laid her back on the bed. I'm no Isaac you know, giving all the blessings to the bringer of the first tasty stew, I'm going to save something for all my children.

Ezinne rose slowly. All? Ma? she gently embraced Ma'Kanu with her eyes shut. She didn't speak for a long time. If I cry at your wake Ma, it will be all your fault. She paused, Have you forgiven every wrong I ever did you?

Of course child.

She hesitated. Can I ask you a last favour Ma?

From behind Ma'Kanu's head, Njide's index fingers flew to her lips in alarm as the old woman ran her fingers through the braids of her youngest foster child. Her voice was trembling with emotion. You may, Ezi, but you mustn't take away the joy you've just given me.

There was a long silence. Somto's searching boot found Ezinne's toes in a gentle tread and when the kindergarten schoolteacher had heaved a breath it was only to shake her head slowly. I'll keep it yet, she whispered.

Somto pulled Ma'Kanu's coverlet up to her chin. Tobe moved to the foot of the bed and gently began to balm her swollen joints. She moaned softly, half in pain, half from the release the massaging brought her. The children settled around their foster mother. There was a certain tension in the air as Ezinne dealt another round of story cards from the shuffled deck. They turned the cards up apprehensively. The words jumped at them: Jewels. Potiskum. Greed. Infidelity. Textiles.

That's easy, declared Ezinne mischievously.

It would be for you, replied Njide. You've told your tale.

Let them *cook*, said Ma'Kanu in an excited rush. Jewels, Potiskum, greed, infidelity, textiles. Don't think of them directly, just let them cook in your mind. Words have their own stories. Listen, they'll tell them to you.

Njide listened to the stark silence for a long moment and gave up. Can't hear anything, she sighed, let's worship awhile. That's part of a wake, eh? Ma?

There was a look of loss in Tobe's eyes as they prepared to enter a world he couldn't fully experience. Do you know this song? Somto asked, describing with his fingers:

> *If you ask me one more time about Jesus*
> *I'll just break down into a song,*
> *Because Jesus Christ has done so much*

That I just can't help myself.

Slowly, they picked up the simple words and joined in, eyes focused on the old woman who lay quietly in state.

The wake continued.

*

Presently, the song ebbed and died quietly. In the peaceful silence that ensued, Ma'Kanu's eyes blinked open and strayed to the *ekwe* drum, which had not spoken in over a decade. A thick film of dust had settled on it, sealing the silence of the goatskin. Her right hand clawed into the wound in her mattress where her flute resided; but the instrument seemed too ashamed to emerge into sight. She was now too breathless for fluting.

Somto rocked to and fro, weighing the silent request. He had turned his back on *vesai* after the problem with Kanu and Udeme. Kanu had been Odozi's champion *vesai* exponent. After the estrangement, music was dead and Somto felt like a banjo without strings... but he wondered how different his intransigence would look, set beside Ma'Kanu's unforgiveness.

The family held its breath as Somto rose and crossed the space that separated him from the accoutrements of *vesai* music. In his youth, every time he approached a drum there was a strange excitement that jumped between him and the instrument. He felt it again, that tingle of low-grade electricity that sometimes numbed one's fingers when the elbow joint was struck between the ulna and the radius bones.

He removed the dust with a moist cotton rag. He tested the tension of the drumskin. He tapped in the stakes carefully with a crowbar. He straddled the drum, pushed it down his laps. Above the family, the zinc rattled apprehensively. Somto tested the drumskin in the air with a tap-tap of his thumbs. His fingers joined in. He played around with his memories, started and didn't finish a flourish, started another and jumped to the end of it. He teased their memories of old tunes, suggesting with his careless fingers that the years had spoiled his art, — or the damp the drumskin, — but his rhythm was still a whisper, the suggestion was still *sotto voce*...

His hands fell silent. Play was over. His eyes opened in earnest. He looked at Ezinne but she shook her head uncertainly.

The drum was the skeleton of Odozi's *vesai* music, but it was the plangent agogo that was the soul of it. It was the agogo that signalled the start and the end, which threaded the argument of the music. The drum controlled the passion and the fervour, but it was the slender iron bell that dictated the pace.

An impulsive Ezinne at the agogo would make all of Odozi within earshot regret the rashness of their Igwe's ostracism, but they would be ruing from their feet, as they responded to the incitement of the percussive idiophone.

Yet, she declined. Whatever Ma'Kanu's expectations, her natural rhythm at the *vesai* seemed out of sync with a wake. Njide moved to Somto's side as her brother hung the heavy agogo by its cord onto a hook that protruded from the rafters. As it swung free, Njide tangled her left leg with a bar stool's. With its stick, she tapped a warning on the flared end of the agogo. A sigh of dust drifted to the ground from the innards of the bell whose peculiar shape and weight gave a surprising range of sound. Ma'Kanu's breath rasped greedily. All Odozi within earshot would regret the rashness of their Igwe's ostracism; but they would do it thoughtfully, from their beds.

The duet commenced.

It was a call-and-reply song. That was the thing about *vesai* music. The drum spoke its piece and the bell replied. No matter how rambunctious the fall of the drumbeat, having spoken, it fell silent until the agogo responded. Ezinne's agogo would start its chant even before Somto's drum was silent and by the end of the duet their music usually fused into a swift medley of excited anticipation.

But Njide was in the saddle. Somto played his heart, an excited rhapsody on the power and the promise of the glory of this present world. Njide let the last juvenile note of his rousing scatter of drumbeats die before uttering her measured dissent, setting the rhythm for the rest of the duet.

In Odozi, call-and-reply was a traditional song form played in an age-bound manner. The renegades of Orphan House had moved the musical conversation of *vesai* in directions that bemused the locals.

Somto's fingers were not shouting, but they were loud. They were the owner of a gruff voice who could not but speak and be overheard. The agogo was half a man's height and its opinion carried weight. Njide's interjections came mostly from the assertive, flared end of the bell; she was the rider of a horse going downhill, a firm hand on the reins. Somto wanted the gallop, Njide wanted the scenery. They worked out a compromise, but the deal-making, the musical struggle between horse and jockey was a wonder to over-hear. Somto had lost none of his rhythm. Njide had acquired new confidence, and a greater depth of emotion.

Ma'Kanu's clawlike hand stretched silently in Ezinne's direction. Her eyes were transfixed on the duet, but her hand held a wood-en flute. Tobe's eyes were rounded as Ezinne reluctantly took the flute. The schoolteacher slipped to the ground and closed her eyes, the flute paused on her lips as she waited for an opening through which to slip into the duet.

The flute's plaintive voice entered the robust argument like a peacemaker wheedling peace in a matrimonial spat. It scurried between the plangent notes of the agogo, nimbly accompanying, agreeing, and at the end, propounding an optimistic plaint of its own. Somto's drum surged forward with renewed gusto, straining at the leash of the sombre bell. The contest continued, the very ten-sion of the struggle for tempo and mood electrified the music.

The sweat stood out on the faces of the musicians. Only Som-to's eyes stood open. The women played with shut eyes, plumbing depths they knew only by feel and not by sight. Njide was already weeping. No one yet knew why, but it would be clear by and by. Her very effort to keep the tears back for Ma'Kanu's sake provoked them the more. There was a reason in her melancholic music that she did not fully understand. When she did, the duet would be over, and her improvisation would begin; and when she was through, there was a fair chance she would no longer be weeping alone.

Suddenly, at the height of Somto's crescendo Njide sounded the two-strike warning from the narrow cup of the bell and Ma'Kanu gasped. Three beats later, Somto crashed from the cliff of sound into a pulsing silence as Njide came down from the stool with the grace of a cat. She sank to the ground beside Ezinne, turning her tear-streaked cheek away from Ma'Kanu as her sister enfolded her in an embrace.

The agogo trembled in the air.

With Njide on the bell, the sessions were short. Somto pulled up his drum ruefully; with quieter, chastened fingers, he picked up again the bare bones of the rhythm they had worked out. While

Ezinne played him into exhaustion, Njide skimmed only the best of his art, leaving him a little hungry for more.

There was no applause from the family. Although it was not a family that overly vocalized thanks, they knew it was not over yet. In traditional *vesai*, the performance was done; but with Njide on the bell, it was only midway. No one knew why she wept while she played: until it was all over, when she translated her agogo's grief.

Ma'Kanu stretched her hand out for Tobe and when he came over on all fours, gripped him tightly as Njide began to croon. Tobe stared intensely at the mysterious drum speaking a language beyond him, and in that intensity, Somto saw again his uncanny resemblance to that hooded giant, the exile, Kanu. The torrents from the instruments had dried into the gurgling rivulet from the ekwe, but the gorges they had cut were firmly etched on the minds of her audience. Somto held true to their course.

He raised his eyes to the low ceiling and saw visions of Potiskum, a Northern Nigeria township he'd visited twice before. Dry and arid, a shade tree in Potiskum had to be more valuable than jewels. Jewels. Greed. Infidelity. Textiles. The story words dropped into the sump of his mind, rattled together briefly, and sank beneath his consciousness as Njide began to sing. Tobe watched Ezinne's fingers as they began to translate Njide's words into sign.

my life is no more mine
my world is no more sweet
where's the road to Yesterday,
back to the Land of Goodness?

mango stored her goodness in the air
and the birds got it.
yam stored her goodness in the ground
and the ants got it.

they got together, mango and yam,
they brought their plaint to God.
year after year, our Father,
my goodness, o my goodness!
those that never laboured ate me,
those that never stored grew fat!

my store has been harvested
by the rapacious
and now I have nothing,
nothing left to keep.

children of the world listen
villagers of my villages, hear me.
this world is no more sweet,
this life is no more mine.
show me the way back to yesterday,
back to the Land of Goodness?

he was cattle when I bought him
but he was truer than my husband
so I kept him, so I nursed him,
so I spoiled and coddled him.
yet, the day of hunger came around
and I boiled and ate him too.

when the world ate my goodness
it was painful.
when I ate the goodness of the world
it was sour.

The Way,
who will take me there?

The thudding of Somto's drum continued for a minute after Njide fell silent and then tapered off. It was done. In exactly the way that he had feared it would happen, a veil of sadness was hung in the air. The spirit of the wake had descended.

Suddenly, Ezinne tensed and turned towards the old door.

There's someone there, she whispered. Somto straightened up from the drum and drew the bolt. There was a moment of apprehension as he drew the door open.

It was only Igwe Nza.

There was a profound silence in Odozi as he stepped quickly into the house. He had a walking stick whose strength he did not need, but he used it with a flourish that gave colour to his promenades. Igwe Nza's real name was Magnus Ofo but no one ever called him that any more. When he became traditional ruler of Odozi he had taken the titular name: Ocean-That-Never-Dries. Occasionally, people did call him 'Ocean', but it was usually with a smile. What most of his subjects called him, even to his face, was Igwe Nza, which in translation meant: 'Sparrow King'. As his voice was no more shrill than any other octogenarian's, it was clearly a reference to his diminutive size.

Close the door, he ordered from the middle of the room. The door was already shut, but his habit of giving orders was one that he gave free rein. He waved his feather-tufted fan around the room. Usually, that was a royal gesture used to acknowledge the greetings and praises of subjects; but from the children of Grace Lodge, there was only a hostile silence.

Ma'Kanu hailed him cheerfully enough. Igweee!

Thank you, he said curtly. He looked from the ekwe drum to the agogo turning slowly in the air and sniffed: When you won't mix with villagers, how will you know how to play *vesai*?

He looked his age, but he was a spare man. There was no flab and the usual wreck of old age was absent. Instead he had an agility uncommon in many fifty-year olds.

Sorry, said Ma'Kanu without evident sorrow, I've no kola, I wasn't expecting visitors at such an *evil* hour.

That is okay, night has become notorious for taking away kola nuts from the homes of misers. The Igwe's eyes strayed towards the settee.

I would have offered you a chair, apologised Ma'Kanu with a straight face, but for those horrible piles of yours, how are they now?

I am fine, said the Igwe angrily, sitting down on a buttock and an elbow, At least it won't kill me.

Ma'Kanu's humour took a poisonous turn. I thought we were both dead. In the Health Centre you swore that no son or daughter of Odozi would set eyes me again, even as a corpse!

I have something important to discuss with you, Ma'Kanu, said the Igwe stiffly, *alone*.

Ma'Kanu was nodding silently, but the smile on her face had frozen into a grimace and her children knew she was battling to mask the pain that sought to embarrass her in front of her tormentor.

You must go now, said Somto quietly, Ma'Kanu has to rest.

I won't be long. He raised his fan and shooed peremptorily, You go away now. Go inside.

You go away yourself, said Ezinne, who had never had such an opportunity to give her sovereign a piece of her mind, how dare you come into my house to order me around.

The Igwe froze. He turned slowly on her. Although he was far from speechless, every moment of silence conveyed a heightened grandeur of rage. They had to admit he *looked* like an Igwe. You are not the one whose witchcraft crazed Orachonsi. You are not the one that ritual killers violated. You must be Ukata's daughter. You *are* the armed robber's daughter.

He allowed the anger to drain from his voice and sighed, The offspring of a snake can't but be long. He turned back to Ma'Kanu with the air of one who had unmasked an unworthy adversary, We are adults. Sensible men don't undress in public just to decide the bigger man. This may be your *house*, but this is my *town*...

You've already done your worst, Ma'Kanu reminded him, mildly enough.

But I can undo it. By morning I can cancel the ostracism...

By morning, I'll be dead, said Ma'Kanu quietly. But if you or your people approach my grave I'll wake up and curse you all.

There was a long silence then Igwe Nza began. If you want the burial of an ass, that is your problem...

...it will be better than the burial of a sparrow.

The Igwe didn't storm out in rage. He drank deeply and painfully of Ma'Kanu's insolence and Somto realised that something very important had brought and kept him there. Before their eyes, the Igwe's arrogance seemed to drain completely. He spoke with a heaviness they had never seen before, in a voice devoid of arrogance.

You must forgive me, Ma'Kanu, I did what I did out of rage. It wasn't that you destroyed Orachonsi's shrine when you burnt down the place, it was that you destroyed me as well.

...that baboon... it was not your...?

Do be *serious* please. My life was hidden in his shrine on the very night you burnt it down. What I want to know now is what happened to the two ashen gourds in the shrine you burnt down? They were about this height, not taller than a three year old, and they were full of money,

What are you talking about? demanded Ma'Kanu.

Igwe Nza sighed. You know Peg Leg the Italian?

The owner of Marble Hill?

Yes, that very day that borned the night that you burnt Ora-chonsi's shrine, we sold Mpete Hill to him. It was more money than I had ever seen before, — and I have worked as cashier for Mines and Power! At my chieftaincy council, we quarrelled over where to keep the money until we... that is, until the next day when we could go to Odozi's bank in Enugu. Finally we agreed for Orachonsi to keep it. It was the one place where thieves have never been. That same night you burnt down the shrine.

You've said that one already.

And I am saying it again! he was raging once again: I am saying we put the money in two ash-colour gourds! They were big like this, like a nine-month pregnancy. Both of them were smelling of palm wine and what I'm asking, Ma'Kanu, is what did you do with them?

Are you suggesting I stole the money? demanded Ma'Kanu, finding strength somewhere for anger.

Igwe Nza was even angrier. When you've been living like a pau-per these past twenty years? Don't be stupid! What I'm asking, *if you will listen*, is whether you saw the gourds when you put fire in the shrine.

Ma'Kanu was incredulous. After *twenty* years? Next, you'll be asking me how many chickens I killed to cook my Christmas lunch of '83! You want me to remember whether there were two particu-lar *gourds* in a witch-doctor's shrine!

Igwe Nza sat back sulkily, squirming as his piles took some pressure. He muttered darkly: He buried it. I know he buried it. No fire could have burnt a gourd buried underground. It's either that or he took it home with him that night.

Njide's voice was gentle. Igwe, it's been twenty years.

Igwe Nza detected the first sympathy since he entered Orphan House and he pointed his fan at her. His eyes were steady as his voice vented a pure distillate of bitterness. *Twenty years of suffering.* Do you know where Orachonsi is now? Do you know how he is living?

I hear, answered Njide indiscreetly, that his present oracle at Abiagha is as famous as the Long Juju of Arochukwu used to be.

Oho! Why won't he be famous when he can now afford to pay informers with my money? Igwe Nza stopped squirming and rose.

He began to pace agitatedly. I dug up many holes myself, with these very hands! All I found were old sacrifices. — And two shopkeepers, at least, complained that his money smelled of palm wine...

His walking stick reared like a cobra and struck the cabin floor venomously. Igwe Nza's hand trembled in the fever of his passion. I would have gone to the police, but the money we gave him to keep was much larger than the official receipt we gave Peg Leg, and the difference could still have made the wizard a wealthy man...

He derailed into a vituperative monologue and Ezinne's hands, which had been interpreting to Tobe, rested modestly in her laps.

This is a Christian home, scolded Ma'Kanu, not unsympathetically. Besides, you're older than I am, you're nearer your grave than your mother's womb and you need God's peace more than a new royal limousine. Forget Orachonsi, who knows, they may still find oil in your domain. What's gone is done, forgive and forget.

Somto widened his eyes in silent delight. He noticed Njide's arched brows. The children exchanged meaningful nods.

You can preach to me! blazed the Igwe. You should have forgiven him and forgotten your daughter instead of burning his shrine! If he took your daughter you'd be cursing him on your deathbed! But it's my money he took! Lookahere, woman, I want you to sign an affidavit for me. All you need to say is that when you burnt the shrine, you had a good look around first, and there was no money there. That will force him to refund my money...

He broke off. Ma'Kanu was laughing tears.

I thought it was Odozi's money, inquired Somto innocently.

Igwe Nza drew himself up and issued a hiss that was liquid with loathing, which seemed to consolidate his venom for Orachonsi with his odium for the residents of Orphan House. Abruptly, he stormed to the door and let himself out. The children drifted to the windows to watch him go. The arrogant steel melted from his spine as soon as he was through the door. He bent almost double as he passed through the cover of Ma'Kanu's profligate flowerbeds. At the gate he looked right and left before he broke abruptly into the street. His walking stick was held silently aloft as he hurried up the hill towards the Old Convent and his palace beyond the Village Square.

Poor man, mused Njide.

He's just as bad as Orachonsi, said Ezinne, He was planning to steal the money for himself.

Yet, he's managed to steal some of my time, said Ma'Kanu, glancing at the clock.

Somto took the hint. He took a deep breath, flexing his fingers for the marathon narration. He wore a confidence that ended just behind his smile. It was alright for Ezinne, who told tales daily. *He was horribly out of shape!* He dredged up the story words once again. He had thrown them, like baited lines, into his seething mind. They came up now wriggling with minnows, not enough meat for a famished Ma' Kanu.

There was nothing to it then but to do the unthinkable and out the most dramatic secret he knew. It was truth that was stranger than fiction anyway. It had greed, jewels and infidelity. He could swap New Bussa for Potiskum and the cutting floor of the New Bussa Leatherworks for the Accounts Department of a Textile Factory. Of course despite all the subterfuge, Udeme would have recognised herself instantly. But she wasn't here to hear the tale. He would smudge the details: ages, names and other give aways, he would entertain the old woman capitally. In the morning she'd be dead, the family would be scattered once again, and his secret would be as safe as it was before.

He cleared his throat nervously. Greed and infidelity! he warned, Potiskum and jewels, textiles! I can feel a story coming.

I can feel two itching ears, came the chorus of expectant voices.

THE DAY OF THE JEWEL

Ψ

Recently, making haste to rise at his boss' approach, Tikum had knocked over his wife's framed photograph, which shattered on the ground. He had grimly swept the shards of glass into the bin. Her shredded photograph followed afterwards.

The real Jorie was, however, more difficult to dispose of.

At forty, Tikum had reached that age when he was desperate for some happiness before he died. Yet, his existence was a double life sentence. The first sentence was served in his home, with Jorie, his hopeless wife of twelve years. The second was the torture at the Potiskum Textile Factory where he worked, in whose cashier's cage his love for the ravishing Nne was imprisoned. From his desk at the Accounts Section, every time Tikum looked up it was to see Nne laugh, talk or simply be her enchanting self.

If only he could change those women around! Put Nne in Jorie's place and Jorie in Nne's place for good! That idea first struck him in a moment of madness; — but once it gained his mind there was no evicting it. It was like one of those idiot jingles that steeped one's mind the way the smell of onions permeated a cook's fingers. However, Tikum had a decent upbringing and twelve responsible years of marriage behind him. He fought this devilish desire with all his might and eventually stopped hankering to change the women around.

It was enough if Nne came into Jorie's place. Jorie could do with herself whatever she pleased.

The problem was to get Nne to take him seriously! On one propitious lunchtime when he found himself on the seat next to her at the canteen he had actually broached the subject of how nice a wife she really would make some lucky man — but she had laughed his words into a bog. She had that way of making a serious thing one had to say suddenly heavy on the tongue. Yet, at forty he didn't have a lot of time.

He once considered getting a skilled propositioner to make his complex intentions clear, but dismissed the idea out of hand. It was thoroughly juvenile, utterly beneath the dignity of a man who already had a marriage almost behind him.

*

Goldsmith Mayomi gave Tikum the perfect idea by putting a show-stopping display in his shop window. The gossip of the stupendous fish set began in the Wrapping Section, which was the department of the factory most conducive to gossip; the women sat in close circles without the roar of machinery that could drown conversation. By lunchtime, the gossip had reached Accounts.

They said it was made of gold and silver — and eyes of precious stones that watched you lustfully, anywhere you stood. They said it was the very perfection of every woman's dream: a necklace, earring, brooch and vanity ring set. They said it was the sort of jewelry whose very possession would give a woman a reputation. And they asked what sin a man could not atone for, by buying it for his wife.

It was clearly beyond the skills of even the wizardly Mayomi, but no one on the factory floor had the wherewithal to inquire closely into the provenance and pedigree of the jewelry.

That very evening Tikum took a scooter-taxi to Mayomi's shop. When he saw the display in the window, he knew he had found the means, not only to catch Nne's attention, but to get her into Jorie's place. It was a stunning jewelry set built entirely of a gold and silver shoal of tiny, beautifully contorted fishes with eyes of precious stones. A woman who was not beautiful in them had no hope of beauty anymore. If he could casually slip the jewelry's suede pouch into Nne's cage — with an eloquent birthday card — he wouldn't have to speak very much thereafter.

It had worked for him before: most of the wooing of his present, useless wife he had done with gifts. — Although nothing anywhere as valuable as the fish set before him.

So he steeled himself and pushed through the heavy, red curtains that kept the poor out of Mayomi's golden world. The smith was a gross and arrogant man. His penchant for peering greedily at gems and rich customers had put a hunch into his back and steel muscles in his beetling eyebrows. His black-and-white perspective on the world made him see things in terms of either gold or dross. A customer who put a finger on his glass displays got it flicked away with the same irritation that a soiled pet was expelled from the owner's lap.

Considering his customer relations Mayomi should have been a pauper. Yet, there was no denying his skill with precious metals — and if you were rich to go with it, you could also insult him as much as you wished and still remain his best customer. Tikum looked from Mayomi's unsmiling features to the jewels. 'Can I hold them?' he asked hoarsely.

'Never,' swore the goldsmith. Tikum blinked. Then he squared up to Mayomi and asked what it would cost to take the jewels home. The goldsmith's eyes dropped slowly from Tikum's perspiring nose to the broken strap of his watch whose life-span had been extended by the cunning stitches of an itinerant shoemaker, and sneered. 'You can't afford it.'

Tikum blinked again, following Mayomi's disdainful eyes down to his scuffed and wounded shoes. Yet, this was by no means the greatest insult a man could get in search of a woman's love. He had prepared a dissimulation for the sake of secrecy; now he redeployed it swiftly to gain credibility. 'It's for my boss at the factory.'

Mayomi remained disdainful, but at least he named his price, whose outrageousness drove Tikum home, divorce banished from his mind.

*

It wasn't that marriage had changed Jorie that much. She was still the same 'Jolly Jorie' Tikum had married; except that now she only laughed at other men's jokes. Even when Tikum's joke caught a smile on her face, it generally soured into a sneer. For all that, he returned from Mayomi's, determined to make his marriage work. Jorie was at the door, dressed for an outing. 'We must talk,' he said with pleading in his eyes.

'Later,' she replied, 'I'm going out.'

He glanced forlornly over her bare ebony shoulder at the bare dining table. Jorie was a gifted cook. When their marriage was young, friends made nuisances of themselves by timing their visits to coincide with mealtimes. These days, only special functions could inspire Jorie to culinary excellence. For her husband she now cooked with her left hand. 'What about dinner?'

Jorie slung her bag petulantly, 'Somebody whose chop money finished last week should ask for dinner more respectfully! There's some beans in the freezer, and better don't finish it if you want any breakfast.'

Although he was asleep by the time she returned, her rebuff wasn't even enough to break his resolve. — That took Miasta losing his thumb to the calendaring machine at the factory. Here's how it happened: The next morning, Miasta was cracking jokes as usual when the calendaring machine picked up an inattentive thumb and smashed it, flesh, bones and blood, into the green textile running majestically on the huge rollers.

For one thumb, the spray of blood was quite spectacular, and Miasta didn't help matters, the way he carried on. The first report that reached Accounts was that Miasta had lost his right arm. The dismayed staff emptied into the sickbay to see poor Miasta. Purely by chance, Tikum was standing behind Nne when the wounded man was borne past, screaming. At the sight and sound of the calamity, Nne swooned — and for those infinitesimal seconds, it was Tikum's powerful arms that preempted another industrial accident.

From then onwards, one face haunted Tikum. It wasn't Miasta's pain-crazed own. It was Nne's, brimming with tender tears in that unguarded moment when she fell into his arms. — And he knew that no price was too much to keep her in those arms forever.

That very lunch hour, he found a sheet and tackled his monthly budget; clearly, something had to give, were he to buy the jewelry. His first sacrifice was the caftan he made every month. If he saved the money religiously, it would take him three years to buy the jewelry. He threw in his weekly suya treat and came down to twenty-eight months. He gave up all hope of riches and chipped in his weekly lottery ticket. An hour every evening doing a trader friend's books could fetch an extra three hundred and fifty naira daily; — and if he added his savings for a new zinc roof for his father's village house, he could actually buy the jewelry in eighteen months.

He was at eighteen months for a long time.

Then he painfully added his weekly league tickets and came down to nine months. He considered reducing Jorie's housekeeping allowance but relented. — If he cut the chop-money, he might not live to conclude the courting of Nne. He racked his brains desperately; nine months was unacceptably long.

Then, despairingly, he remembered his 28-inch colour TV.

Six months back he had hocked his pride and joy to a pawnbroker to pay a family levy. His TV was due back home that month end. Giving up both football and TV at the same time was a grievous sacrifice. He glanced at Nne's empty cubicle. On one wall was pinned her mother's photograph. Within weeks, he could be on that wall. It was a worthwhile sacrifice. He figured in the secondhand value of his TV and came down to sixteen weeks! He could have the jewels by Nne's birthday!

That very evening, he withdrew his savings for his father's roof and called at Mayomi's with his first installment. As soon as the goldsmith sensed a sale, he became the soul of hospitality, ushering Tikum solicitously into an inner room. There were spectacular catalogues mounted on the walls and a table in a corner, set for tea. He disdained business until his wife, whose nature was as genuinely cheerful as his was brooding, had served them both from a steaming pot of zobo tea.

Mayomi flinched when he heard the duration of the installment plan. He took the canister of sugar that the sweating Tikum had been using rather liberally, made a token sprinkle over his mug and set it down proprietarily next to him. 'Four months? No,' he said. Then he repeated emphatically, with the indignation of a caretaker who, having accepted a chimpanzee for a tenant, was now requested to baby-sit infant chimps, 'No, no, no!'

'But consider my wife, Sir Mayomi...'

'Whether it's for your wife or your boss is irrelevant! My masterpiece? Eighteen-carat gold? Electroplated silver? Precious stone insets? A thousand times no!'

'But consider, Chief Goldsmith, it's been in your window one month already...'

'... making me famous! And I won't hide it in a drawer waiting for your miserable installments! A thousand times...'

'But consider, revered jeweler, if I miss an installment,' Tikum took a deep breath, ' all I've paid is yours.'

'Do you take me for a moneylending RAT,' thundered Mayomi from his feet, 'that you bait me with your measly money? Those jewels pull in more business for me than all the installments you can pay in a year! Tell your boss and wife I said no!'

'A thousand times,' mumbled Tikum hoarsely, slinking into the night. He was sweating from the tea and the disgrace and his money burned shamefully in his pocket. He passed a miserable night tossing beside Jorie.

*

That Friday he was rude to Nne; and when Rajeev the Accounts Director passed his desk, by pretending not to see him, he procured not to rise. As things went, that was rank folly. When old Oti was fired last Christmas there wasn't much anybody could say against him, except that he'd laughed the day the boss' wig fell off.

The weekly Christian fellowship in the accounts hall had to be a quick one, for the owners of the factory were Buddhists. Although the union had wrested that once weekly right to pray during the lunch-break, the prayers had to end well within half an hour and they sometimes took on the spirit of a hundred metres dash. As the onsets sped, Tikum, who attended it by default because he was too depressed for lunch, realised it was a mistake to remain behind: his new marriage was the first major step in his life that he had not dared pray about.

'Pray, brethren pray!' urged the lay pastor strenuously, as the fellowship approached its climactic Amen. For the first time, Tikum tried to pray about Nne, about Jorie, about himself; but it was hopeless, completely impossible. What he desperately wanted was so irreconcilably at odds with what God unequivocally instructed. 'But You know I'm unhappy!' He ended up telling God miserably.

The brethren dispersed, just as the clean-shaven Rajeev strolled past the hall, checking that nobody was praying on time that he was paying for. Right afterwards a determined little woman entered, nonplussing a harassed orderly who was grumbling that the lunch-break was almost over. She was already sitting in front of Tikum before the depressed clerk looked up. 'Good afternoon,' she smiled, her fat cheeks dimpling.

'What do you want?' demanded Tikum truculently.

'You weren't so rude yesterday,' she remarked, 'as you drank my tea.' Tikum's eyes widened in recognition and he hurried her to a private corner of the junior staff reception.

'I'm sorry,' he apologised. 'I was in a bad mood.'

'I perfectly understand,' replied the lady. She was short, even for a woman; but her mischievous eyes couldn't stop winking, and her lips always seemed in the process of making another smile, — all of which made her peculiarly friendly, even for a woman. 'My husband told me everything. He was so furious!'

'So what did I do to make him furious?' demanded Tikum, blowing a top that he might have blown, to better effect, the night before. 'So a poor man can't buy gold again?'

'Exactly what I asked him.' Her eyes softened as she studied Tikum. 'You know how long I've been a goldsmith's wife?'

'No,' said Tikum guardedly. He was unsure where this was leading and afraid for his job as the minute hand poised to strike 2 pm.

'...A considerable time,' she said, generalising just in time. Her eyes glazed over, '— and in all that time I never owned jewels like that fish set...' she clapped her tiny hands determinedly, 'No! I must stick to the point! The point is this: in all that time I've never seen a man like you, sacrificing so much for love. In fact I'll tell you something you must promise never to tell my husband.'

'What?' asked Tikum unhappily, reluctant to share anything with the goldsmith's wife to the exclusion of her massive husband.

'I told him,' she said vengefully, 'that I wished you were my husband.' Tikum could not speak. 'I tell you,' she continued passionately, seizing Tikum's elbow securely, 'in all my years as a goldsmith's wife, I have never seen such a romantic gesture. Four months of such... supreme sacrifice for such a ... heavenly gift. — Your wife is blessed, young man.'

'Madam,' began Tikum desperately, for it was now 2 pm; if Rajeev passed just then that would be half his day's wages down the drain.

'My name is Ola,' she scolded, 'and let me tell you something, I may be small, but when I want something, I get it. You know what I said to my husband? I said to him,' she winked, 'Mayo, you're giving that boy those silly beads of yours — on his terms. You know what he said? No, no, no! A...'

'...thousand times no.' Tikum inched towards the exit, half-dragging the insistent woman.

'Exactly. That's how he started anyhow, but by 2 am this morning he said "Yes"!'

Tikum whipped around ecstatically, grabbing Ola's own elbows. 'Yes?'

'Look at that smile!' declared Ola with childish delight, as Nne hurried past from her lunch, amused eyebrows arching at the unexpected scene. 'When I went to sleep at 2 am, I said to myself, Ola, you're going to make two lovely smiles this morning!'

Tikum stopped smiling. 'Two smiles?'

'Your wife,' she explained. 'Now, if you just give me your first install-ment you've got yourself a contract. I'd have been here all morning but I...'

'You've told my wife?' groaned Tikum in despair.

'I can't until you tell me where I can find her,' said Ola fishing out an address book.

Tikum sighed in relief and his voice dropped into a conspiratorial whisper, 'I will, but you must promise never to mention this to her...'

Ola's eyes grew round as she hugged herself. 'It's a surprise? Oh, but you're so romantic.' Tikum was already gone. He got his deposit out of his drawer and into Ola's hands in a matter of moments and the gold-smith's wife left for home, mission accomplished.

*

Fifteen weeks passed, a blur, with Ola coming in every week to col-lect what money Tikum had put away. She noted each deposit diligently in her small notebook, squeezing his palm encouragingly when it was small, winking when it was sizeable. The goldsmith's wife developed a proprietary interest in this romantic project that rivalled Tikum's in pas-sion, and she mopped up any loose cash that might tempt the clerk to squander any of his hard-won savings.

Then came that Monday in late August that Tikum got his strange visitor. It was also the day Nne called him a goat. At 1 pm Tikum had hurried into the reception. Instead of the overdue Ola, a sullen goldsmith confronted him with the seething accusation: 'You are seeing my wife?'

Tikum stared, mesmerised, at the gray wire-brush of Mayomi's bristling moustache. 'Ah, well, technically, yes I see her every week — but not in the sense...'

'There's no "but" in this matter. You're either seeing her or not. Since you are, what I have to tell you is: Stop! Okay? Stop, stop, stop! Okay? A thousand times, stop!'

He got to his feet. Tikum rose as well, trying to work up enough self-righteous anger to confront the intimidating goldsmith, 'Listen, I...'

But, Mayomi was raging, with the air of someone who had decided, damn it all, to boast. 'And let me tell you something, Accounts Clerk, I'm a rich man. I employ a chartered accountant. I totally provide for my wife. I don't just feed her romantic dreams. And I have no apologies to anyone.' Then he stalked arrogantly away.

A desperate Tikum trailed him, his anger project in ruins, hissing in a secretive whisper. 'I'm collecting the jewels next week?'

Mayomi wheeled majestically. 'I am a Japanese-trained, government-licensed metallurgist and goldsmith. I am not a hawker. If you want to buy my jewels you know where my showroom is.' Then he walked away.

Subsequently, Tikum thought frantically over every word and nuance of his conversation with the goldsmith and realised that something was terribly wrong. Already it was ten days since Ola's last visit, her longest absence ever. Although another four days still separated Tikum from his next payday and the final installment, suddenly he was filled with dreadful suspicions. A clammy spirit of desperation swamped him and he knew he had to claim his jewels immediately.

The only way to raise the balance that day was by borrowing, yet none of his friends could make a loan for anything more substantial than a lunch... It was at this point that his eyes strayed, unfortunately, to Nne's cage. That was how come, eventually, she called him a goat.

Following the Tunde Embezzlement, the factory employed only female cashiers as the bosses believed them a less fraudulent sex. Each cashier carried a cash imprest in her safe, which was retired every Friday. If Nne was certain to get the money before the Chief Accountant reconciled her books on Friday evening, she could safely make the loan. Yet, in the company's eyes it was a crime of such heinous dimensions that only Tikum's certainty that the fish set was in danger propelled him to stand, at 1.15 pm, by the door of Nne's cage.

Nne was dabbing on lipstick, which vaguely annoyed Tikum. Wasn't she merely stepping out for lunch? He opened the cage door and slipped inside. Privacy. They were still in the full view of the almost empty office but if they kept their voices low they could still have a totally private conversation. She didn't.

'Ha! Tikus Tikum! Is this a rape attempt?'

The problem with Nne was that she could never be serious. Tikum ignored the sally and told her exactly what he wanted; leaving out only the fact that the loan was to help buy her the most precious jewels in Potiskum. When he finished he was gratified to see on her face, a look of appropriate gravity. In the silence they could hear the dice scatter on the ludo glass as Manuel killed his lunch hour with solitary games.

'Who sent you?' she asked eventually. Although her voice was satisfactorily low it had a hysteric rattle that disconcerted Tikum.

'How, what do you—'

She plunged her finger into his chest so savagely that, weeks later, all he had to do to feel pain lance through his heart was glance at her. 'Whose voucher have I stopped in this company that you want them to sack me? Whose promotion am I blocking? What removed Tunde Aseju from this very cage? What's he doing at Township Prison at this very moment?'

It was quite clear at that stage that Nne wasn't dealing. Yet, Tikum shared with Oba Ovonramwen of nineteenth century Benin Kingdom a tragic inability to enforce total and expeditious surrender in his armies. Tikum found his mouth whispering, trying to cue Nne to lower her own rising voice. 'Tunde put his imprest into the lottery. Imagine that, the lottery! I am only asking you for a loan till Friday. Is there anything risky in Friday? Common four days! Aren't you the cashier that pays my salary? You can just deduct your loan — plus interest if you like — and give me the balance. I promise you won't regret it, in fact, if only you knew...'

That was when she called him a goat. He suspected she called him other names as well, but he fled as soon as she erupted. As he bolted from the hall he was thankful that by then the only person left in the office was Manuel, who usually ran out of lunch money the day after payday.

'You're a goat!' shrieked Nne furiously, beside herself with rage. 'Kai! See his horns; see his tail, devil like you! Go and tell your medicine man that the juju he gave you couldn't blind me! Yes, Nne should now donate her skull for another man to use for a soup bowl! I don't blame you anyway; it's my fault for talking to every Tomandjerry in this company. When a woman stays too long in the market, even lizards will come out and haggle for her wares...'

'What happened?' asked Manuel curiously, his dice suspended in the *cap of an aerosol.*

'Did I complain to you that something happened?' hissed Nne derisively as she swept out of the office without so much as a glance at Manuel. 'He doesn't have money to eat but he has ears for other people's business!'

*

A goat? That will give you the best jewels in Potiskum? In the canteen, that was what Tikum could simply not understand, as he ate his tuwo with a pounding heart. Why couldn't she simply have said 'no'? Any man in her place would quietly have said 'no', and if he felt too strongly, even, a million 'no's.

His heart felt as though it was still pinned to the wall by the javelin of Nne's index finger, and he wondered apprehensively if that was a presentiment of future matrimonial violence. Why did women have to have scenes? Now with Nne as cross as she was, somehow he had to appease her before Friday when he presented the jewels...

The thought of the jewels refocused his mind on his problem: first, he had to get them! Where was that Ola? How could he raise cash immediately? Tikum was so preoccupied that he unconsciously took a second wrap of tuwo from the basket, thus having his first full lunch in the ten days since he had started to starve himself to save for a suitable birthday dinner.

*

Even stranger things were happening at home. Tikum had desperately been trying to provoke a major quarrel as the day of the jewels drew nearer. Jorie was staying out later than ever, but by the time he worked himself up to a murderous rage, she would enter the house practically on her knees; and his anger would escape in an impotent 'Where have you been all evening!' Although he now felt sure there was another man, he was too squeamish to look for the evidence. What he wanted was to stand at a distance and work up a mountain of rage from which, self-righteously, to kick her out within the next few days.

That was proving difficult.

By Tuesday evening, unable to bear the three days left until payday, Tikum visited his elder sister. A nurse at the Potiskum Health Centre, she was in far more desperate straits than he because where Tikum was childless her husband had wanted a boy so badly that he had died after her fifth daughter. She regularly warned Tikum that rather than make more children he was welcome to one or two of hers. Yet, such was Tikum's desperation that he broached the issue of a loan with her.

The embattled nurse, whose salary was a couple of months in arrears, began to wail as soon as Tikum mentioned the figure of the loan. She rose and fled to her altar where she clutched a figurine of Mary and the child Jesus and fell to her knees, weeping.

Tikum finally shut his mouth and hurried to console her as his nieces ran in from the yard, fear in their eyes, 'You didn't hear me, Sister, I only asked for a loan, till Friday.'

'Did you kill somebody? Do you have to bribe the police? Why do they want so much money?'

'No Sister, I...'

'Jorie's mother died? Oh God, PAPA! It's Papa isn't it? Papa is dead?'

The girls began to wail as well. Tikum found himself consoling mother and daughters over a nonexistent bereavement, and he was losing his temper. 'For goodness sake Sister, no!'

'Then you've embezzled office money! Tell the truth, Tikky, on the gentle heart of my husband, of our dear mother, how long do you have to refund it? And what put you up to such a thing?' She reached behind the photograph of the Holy Family for an ancient leather purse, which she opened and shook out. Two forlorn notes fluttered out, snatched from the air by two quick little fists. 'That's all I have in the world and my Tikky is in trouble!' She dissolved into a fresh paroxysm of sobs. 'Tikky that has never asked me for a kobo is in trouble and, ekpini, I don't have!'

It took him another hour to persuade her to forget that he ever mentioned a loan. Yet, as they saw him off he could see from her eyes that she was going to light a candle for him on her altar as soon as he left.

*

Tikum trudged home, wishing he were going instead to the goldsmith's with the balance of the price of the jewelry in his pocket. He clenched one fist after the other, pummelling one palm after the other. He kept seeing visions of the goldsmith's wife wearing his jewelry. He was a rack of test tubes full of potent distillates of love and hate, liberty and entrapment. He had to walk carefully to prevent a spill that could set off a fearful explosion.

He pushed open his door and his nostrils were assailed by a dizzyingly delicious smell that told him that Jorie was cooking for the P.T.A. again. He thought he heard the sound of breaking glass as his emotions coalesced into a blinding anger.

Usually when she cooked for her functions she left him pediatric-sized scrapings in the pot. On this day, despite his keen hunger, the very thought of eating Jorie's delicious leftovers choked him. Jewels or no jewels he resolved to go out and eat a good, self-indulgent meal — on credit, if need be. He stalked into his room, grunting a response to Jorie's friendly greeting from the kitchen. As he tore off his work clothes, his eyes fell on the gap in the shelf where, by the grace of God, the most beautiful china in the house, an exotic double dish set, ought to have been.

He froze.

'Jorie!' he thundered in a murderous rage. He rushed for the kitchen, stumbling over his briefs until he kicked them off. 'JORIE!'

It was his Distinguished-Service Award for diligence! He'd warned her: 'No public functions' but she'd never listen! Then came the wedding in which one was broken! He'd pulled her ear lobe again! Never again, he'd warned her! Never, Never, NEVER! The anger was a potent intoxicant in his bloodstream and he knew that today he was going to beat her silly. Today he was going to throw her out! 'JORIE!!'

He slammed the kitchen door into the shelf and the cleaver and three bulbs of onions bounced into the sink. 'Yes dear?' she said, straightening up from garnishing a side-plate of chopped fruits and presenting a defenceless cheek like one expecting a kiss. Perhaps it was the illogic of that defenceless cheek. Perhaps it was the sight of his precious china brimming with a mouth-watering ukazi soup, which was steaming somnolently on a dining-table set for two. Whatever it was, it punctured Tikum's rage all over again and his descending fist ended up, despairing fingers, clumsily not-quite-caressing his wife's neck.

'Hungry and angry as usual,' she giggled, with a glimmer of her old jollity, 'well, you're not eating my food undressed like that!'

*

It was payday and Tikum was in deep trouble. He'd never been in such a panic in his life. He was a coward, and didn't care who knew it now. He didn't have the heart to say to a wife who had done him no recent wrong: it's all over; pack your things and go. He could say it only in the throes of rage and having said it, he would then steel his heart against the dangerous tears of her sex and turn to a happier life.

It was payday! He watched Nne narrowly through the morning hours. For the first time since he had taken her martial finger in his chest, she had smiled at him as he warily signed for his pay envelope in her window; and when he counted his wages, it was a hundred naira too much. Mystified, he had returned the surplus.

Nne hailed Salamotu who worked in the cage halfway across the hall. Along with half the clerks in the accounts hall, they had a good laugh at Tikum's expense. Afterwards, she turned patiently to him, addressing him the way one might counsel a naive schoolboy. 'I've worked here eight years, Holy Tikus, I have underpaid people many times but I've never overpaid a single time. Go count your money again.' He turned away sheepishly, speculating that perhaps he was a beneficiary of a complex, feminine apology for an excess of emotion for which there could be no direct acknowledgement.

It was the day of the jewels! Although now he had the final installment, the tension of the past four months had taken its toll and he now lacked the mental energy for the war of nerves at the goldsmith's shop. He lacked the conviction for the presentation of the jewels, the confidence for the basking in Nne's amazement and the casual making of a dinner date. He lacked the stomach for the messy, emotional scene that evicting Jorie had come to be. The morning came and went with Rajeev's moustache twitching angrily at Tikum's careless figures.

The siren for 1 pm screamed from the factory floor. Manuel was the first person through the doors. Tikum was the last. He had no appetite for lunch. He drifted to the junior staff reception and, at 2 pm, drifted back to his desk. Once again, Ola had not shown.

By 5 pm, he had psyched himself up. He was finally, angry enough. For an accounts clerk, love had made him pretty foolish: he had not taken a single receipt from the goldsmith's wife. Yet, nobody was going to drink his sweat and blood and go scot-free. He took his final payment and pushed a new penknife down a sock. Then he hailed a motorbike taxi for the short trip to the goldsmith's shop.

The jewels were not in the window-display. Tikum grimly pushed his way through the curtain. Inside, Mayomi was intimidating a young couple into a choice of wedding rings. Tikum's heart was pounding as he shouted: 'Where are my jewels?'

'In your house, I presume,' snarled Mayomi. 'You're standing in my shop.'

Tikum pushed a fistful of money in the goldsmiths face, but his anger faltered in the face of the monstrosity of his situation. His voice, which started out a growl, ended up a whine. 'I've paid fourteen installments on the fish set, this is the balance... don't you remember?'

'Ah, cash,' smiled Mayomi solicitously, extending a large, avaricious hand. A calculator slipped out of his breast pocket. 'fourteen installments eh? Let's see your receipts then...'

Mayomi was tugging at the desperate wad of currency, but Tikum's shaking hand did not release it. The middle-aged clerk's voice was shaking as well, 'First show me the fish set; and where's your wife as well? She didn't give me any receipts herself!'

Mayomi flared and dropped his voice into a threatening hiss, 'Keep my wife out of this, you hear me...' but at that precise moment, his eyes strayed back to the young couple inching towards the exit. Releasing the money, he pushed Tikum towards the catalogue room and snapped, 'Wait there till I finish with more important customers.' Then he transferred his dubious charm to the timid couple. As Tikum walked into the other room, Mayomi was explaining to his prospective customers, in a not-so-confidential whisper, 'Romantic fool!'

'Fool at forty,' muttered Tikum in agreement, sinking bitterly behind the small dining table. He put the money on the table and stared at the gray safe in the wall as he listened to the goldsmith's insolent voice alternate with the wheedle of the prospective bridegroom.

The inner door opened and Ola walked slowly to the head of the table. 'I heard your voice from the bedroom,' she said. A smile flickered in the corners of her mouth and died of embarrassment. Her lips tried again, 'I knew today was payday, I knew you would come.'

Tikum recognised the necklace on her bosom and came to his feet, his voice dripping with fury. 'So this was what it was all about? You were lusting after the jewels yourself.'

Despite her embarrassment, her voice was defiant. 'What woman can look at those jewels and not desire them, how much more a goldsmith's wife? I told you Tikum, when I want something, I get it.'

The blatant confirmation of the fraud was too much for Tikum. His fingers opened and closed. Yet, his instincts had been compromised by a lifetime of chilvary and despite the provocation of the jewels on show, the mechanics of a knife assault on the petite goldsmith's wife utterly defeated him. 'All that posing was a front,' he said bitterly. 'So much for your romantic nonsense, "I want to make smiles!" You just picked up the jewels and fled.'

She hung her head. 'I am sorry. I just couldn't face you again after I broke my word to you...'

The goldsmith's roar issued through the curtains, 'Go on, try a blacksmith, and if you want them even cheaper, try your panel-beater!' The trembling curtains parted as he shuffled into the inner room, breathing heavily. At the sight of a more substantial target, Tikum willed himself to stoop for his weapon. Yet, the goldsmith was twice his weight, with an orangutang's arm span. In the close intimacy of the inner room the clerk knew he might never live to straighten up with his weapon.

'Cheapskates!' muttered Mayomi darkly, walking to his safe. 'How a sensible girl can be preparing to marry a man who can't afford decent rings, I don't know! What's happening to girls of nowadays?'

'They are falling in love, darling,' said the little woman taking her husband's hand, 'and unless you realise that your job is to beautify love, one day I'm just going to throw open your doors and give out all your jewels.'

For the first time, Tikum saw the goldsmith laugh as he glanced at Ola's little notebook and popped it back into the safe. Tikum was embarrassed, just to hear it. For it was not the guffawing of a man out with the boys. It was the chortling of a man jesting with his sweetheart, and neither the goldsmith nor his wife could be a day under sixty. Tikum let his eyes fall to his scuffed and wounded shoes as the elderly couple sported.

'Now, Accounts Clerk,' said Mayomi, letting the amusement drain from his voice, 'here's your merchandise. Now let me check your balance.' He dropped a black suede pouch on the table and flipped open the beauty of the complete fish set into view. With the same motion, he reached for the money in front of Tikum.

'No, no, no!' said Ola in a fair imitation of her husband's voice, 'you promised to waive the balance.'

'Come on, Lolly,' wheedled the goldsmith greedily, he took the money and his expert fingers swiftly sorted it for counting, 'the money is here, you can see it's no trouble at all for him. Besides, I never promised him a discount, whereas he owes me this money.'

'You gave me the discount on his behalf,' said Ola firmly, tugging the money from her husband's reluctant fingers and pressing it into Tikum's flabbergasted ones. 'And having broken my word to Tikum I have to make it up to him, on my honour.'

'Honour!' said the goldsmith disgustedly. He took the money from Tikum's nerveless fingers and fanned it, preparatory to counting. 'Honour! We're talking about business here Lolly,' he waved the money, 'you're looking at my profit margin here!' He swiftly began to count, holding the money above his head and well out of Ola's modest reach.

'And we're talking about redeeming the honour of a goldsmith's wife who has broken her word to a customer,' said Ola, digging into her husband's unprotected sides. Presently, he began to laugh and wriggle, lowering his arms to ward off Ola's dextrous fingers. Tikum looked away prudishly as Ola reclaimed his money. 'And talking about profit margins, Mayo, I know your cost price!'

'Now let's be reasonable Lolly darling,' urged the huge goldsmith following his little wife around the small room, 'what word of honour are we talking about here?' he reached for her but she dodged away, 'So you promised the boy you won't tell his wife and you told her? So what? Who cares? Ask him, see if he cares!'

'It's not just telling her, you philistine!' laughed the goldsmith's wife, tripping backwards around the room, pushing back her husband's nose with a finger when he came too close, 'It's spoiling his surprise! It's letting her come here every blessed night for the last one week! It's drinking her joy as she tried on the jewels in my own mirror! It's enjoying all those tears she shed, all that gossip I winkled out about her adorable husband, how he wooed her with gifts, his incredible sacrifice for the jewels... and then her pledges, how the rest of her life she would...'

'Ya, ya, ya,' snorted the goldsmith impatiently, 'so she cried for you, so what? She'll still cry when he gives it to her, you'll see! She'll be crying for the next few weeks, I know that kind of tears, they never finish. That's not why I should lose all this money! After all, he missed last week's payment. I ought to forfeit all his payments! Give it here, Lolly baby...' suddenly he lunged at her, she feinted and slipped out of his grasp, passing the money deftly to Tikum who had the presence of mind to make it disappear before the heavy goldsmith could spin around. She laughed as she continued her playful circuit of the room, empty hands still behind her back.

'Put my honour aside then, Mister Goldsmith, don't you owe this boy something then?'

'Something? For what?'

'For rejuvenating your marriage! I owe him my jewels...'

'NONSENSE!' roared the goldsmith furiously, rearing to his full height. 'A thousand times, NONSENSE! I bought you your jewels, in cash, not in miserable installments!' With that he swept up his wife who happily allowed herself to be caught, latching onto him with both hands. Her eyes fell on the open-mouthed Tikum and she exclaimed in mock affront.

'Peeping Tom! What are you still doing here? Are you a referee or something?' At which Tikum scooped up his jewels and fled the goldsmith's shop, his murder weapon still sheathed.

Yet, he paused on the threshold. If he took another bike, he could reach the factory just as the cashiers finished balancing their books with the Chief Accountant. Then Ola giggled again behind him; and he considered the dizzying possibilities of a rejuvenated marriage and fled home to Jorie.

Ψ

Ma'Kanu's eyes were closed when Somto finished and they were not sure she was still awake. Then her eyes fluttered open and fastened on Somto.

You didn't like my story, he said breathlessly. It was a statement rather than a question. Her body language had spoken volumes as he rounded up his tale. He felt more exhausted than he usually felt after a full shift on the rig.

It's nice, she grudged, damning him with faint praise. Oh, it's got everything: plenty of jewels and Potiskum, some greed, a hint of textiles, and infidelity you need a magnifying glass to see.

Somto is a bashful one, said Njide lightly, wondering at the irritation in Ma'Kanu's manner.

It's a good story, repeated Ma'Kanu more insistently,

But something's wrong, said Somto tightly. He had known her too long not to read her accurately.

The sixth ingredient. It was wagging a finger in Ezinneamaka's story. It's shaking a Bible in yours.

A *sixth* ingredient? asked Tobe, Have I missed something?

Your stories run like folktales and your morals are jumping at me. She grumbled, sounding almost childish in her pique. I asked for stories — don't know if you're storytellers or preachers.

I don't understand, said Njide picking her words carefully. She was looking at her foster mother but her fingers were enunciating slowly for Tobe's benefit, if they were preaching at you, what was their sermon?

Ask them! said the old woman uncomfortably. They're right here!

That's not what you taught us, accused Njide. You always said the storyteller's job ends with his applause. Afterwards it was for his audience to see in it what they could — or wanted to.

She was silent for a while, fretting with the story cards. When she spoke, her voice was bitter: Ezinneamaka's story says not to trammel true love: let Rekia marry whomsoever she wants. SomtoChukwu preaches forgiveness — Tikum returns to his wife. His sacrifices rejuvenate his family. He pays a new bride price for joy to flow again. She paused. Her children did not stir. You know what I say to that?

Four people shook their heads. Furiously, she dealt five cards, and bunged the rest into the old purse. She opened her own card and laid it face upwards. It read, Ikot-Ekpene. She continued: It's one thing to forgive a wife who breaks your china and serves you the portion of a dog, but there are things that run too deep for forgiveness.

Somto sighed heavily. He opened his card slowly. It read, Caretaker. He spoke gently, hoping that his sarcasm didn't break the magic of a *logical* discussion on the biggest crisis in the family. Like Orachonsi's theft of Igwe Nza's money?

Ma'Kanu seemed to flinch as her sharp words to Igwe Nza struck back at her.

And what is it about your past that you can't share with your children? demanded Ezinne, who had indulged numerous teenage daydreams of a fairy grandmother, Margarita. What can be that shameful? What can be that terrible? What can be that unforgivable?

Njide bowed her head ruefully as the bitter judgment of the children descended once again on the old woman. This wasn't what she'd planned. She selected and raised a card, trying to draw attention back to the story-fest. It read, Papa. She placed it beside Ezinne's open card, which read, Lost and Found. Ma'Kanu took a deep breath. Prop me up on my pillow, she exhaled, I'll tell a tale.

Bless me first Ma, said Somto going to his knees.

No, declined Ma'Kanu harshly, your tale isn't complete till mine is told. Prop me up. You always wanted to know your parents, how you ended up in Grace Lodge.

Somto was thunderstruck. You told me you didn't know them, he whispered, that I was given to you by a missionary who has since returned to Ireland.

I lied to protect your feelings. I lied to protect your mother's secret. But I won't take the lie to my grave. Everyone else knows their story. SomtoChukwu, God will give me strength to tell you one more tale for the road. You've preached to me in Tikum's tale, I'll just tell you some true history in mine. We'll skip the story cards now. The only ingredient of my tale will be truth. And at the end, if you're still preaching forgiveness, I'll listen – and *then* I'll bless you.

SILENCE IN HEAVEN

Ψ

The worst anyone could say about Madam-Put-More was that she was money-mad; — and you had to be really cross, even to say that. For although she was money-mad, she had such a consummate skill for dispossessing her clients of their money that her victims were more wont to applaud than berate her. She was a practical sort of woman. When customers kept discovering flies, roaches and sundry insects in their unquestionably delicious soups, she'd yanked out the 65-watt bulbs in her restaurant and replaced them with 25-watt romantic-blue candle-bulbs. No further roach-sightings were ever reported at Madam-Put-More's.

Her sense of the pragmatic had made her what she was: owner of probably the most successful restaurant in... shall we say, Ebene.

Then came the day she sold her largest meal ever. Of course, 'sold' isn't quite the word — but now, I'm getting ahead of my story. Here's what happened. It was about seven in the evening, that time when closing shops and grumbling stomachs conspired to sell the most meals. That evening, the favourite seats outside the restaurant had been taken when the Stranger arrived.

He was tall, well-built, and slung a weathered travelling bag on one shoulder. His clothes seemed decent enough, though well-travelled. Madam-Put-More glanced at him without much excitement. He had no potbelly and didn't look particularly rich. She sized him up as a one-time-only 'rice-without-fish' customer, the kind that held no prospect of a repeat custom, the kind that bought the basic meal and left no tip...

Anyhow, not to get ahead of my story, the Stranger sauntered into the restaurant, greeting everyone jauntily. He told Chief Gbedu, as though they were equals, that since the Chief had a view of the road, should a yellow Mercedes with a Rastafarian behind the wheel drive by, he should be sure to wave it down, as his travelling companion had stopped in the Esso next door to fill up their fuel tank.

On the threshold of the inner section, the Stranger stood stock still, and seemed to enter into a trance. Before him, a mechanic with a toothpick in his mouth was waiting to leave. Behind him, the waitress, Tamara, was waiting with an empty jug of water. He raised his hand and when he got relative silence, solemnly intoned: 'I can smell the blood of the angry dead.'

'You don't need a nose to tell that the goats and chickens in my soup pots died angrily,' said Madam-Put-More from her table. 'You're blocking my entrance.'

He did not move. 'I'm not talking about your chickens, I'm talking about men.' His eyelids were fluttering as he continued, modestly enough, 'It's a gift I have, this spiritual sense of smell. I can sense the emotional essence of a town, just like that. I felt this right from Ebene bridge, but it's very strong now, very strong now.' He turned slowly; he'd caught the attention of the restaurant and he seemed to know how to use attention. His finger strayed uncertainly, until it was pointing resolutely at the town hall. 'Fire,' he pronounced heavily. 'That's how they died. Can't you sense it?'

There was a dramatic silence in the restaurant, until Chief Gbedu sucked skeptically on a crushed drumstick. 'There's been no death by fire in this town, and I've lived here more than sixty years.'

The Stranger hissed impatiently, 'Sixty years! I'm talking two-hundred-year-old smells here!' He seemed to snap out of his trance, 'Is that stewed crab I'm smelling?' he waved his hand at Madam-Put-More. 'Come, is this a restaurant or what? Where's the food?'

He took a table for two. He had a way with the serving staff and got even Tamara, who never smiled with the customers, to laugh several times before his order was ready.

That order caused a stir in the restaurant. In a casual voice, he ordered six wraps of pounded yam, with a plate of egusi soup served with extra stockfish, extra turkey and extra bush meat, as well as six wraps of amala with another plate of drawsoup served with extra chicken, extra fresh fish, extra snail and four large pieces of beef. It was an order to task a gluttonous foursome.

'For you alone?' The unflappable Tamara had cried.

'Am I crazy?' the Stranger had retorted with the air of one who had just been insulted. Frankly, I think he was, but then, as I said, that would be getting ahead of my tale. 'How can one man finish all that?' he snapped, 'Serve them in two trays and cover one, my Rasta friend will be here soon.'

That was how Tamara presented the Stranger with the largest meal Madam-Put-More's restaurant had ever served. She obediently brought the second tray and covered it on the place-mat beside the Stranger. She also brought some takeaway plastic plates, which the Stranger waved away contemptuously.

Madam-Put-More was in her usual place beside the entrance door, from where she kept an eye on both Tamara, who served the main restaurant, and Etuna, who did some cooking and served the open-air section. The Stranger's order had rubbished her original estimation of him. Despite Chief Gbedu's wealth and substantial potbelly, his normal order was three wraps of pounded yam with chicken in drawsoup. Feeling obliged to be cordial to such a substantial customer, she had observed, in a voice laced with professional admiration: 'Are you a boatman? My mother taught me that nothing makes an appetite like paddling against a strong current.'

The man had laughed heartily as he finished unwrapping his six helpings of pounded yam. 'I'm a traveller; the heat and dust of the road can make a sharper appetite than any river, I can tell you.'

'Seems like you've been on the road a long time.'

'And I'm going to be there all my life.'

It was Madam-Put-More's turn to laugh. 'You don't know what you're saying. A man's got to work to eat and if you are going to be on the road all your life you've either got to be a vagrant or a very rich fellow.'

'Exactly,' agreed the Stranger without further elaboration. He swallowed a particularly large helping of pounded yam and asked, as he chased it down with a tiny sip of water, 'you want to know how I received my mission?'

'What mission?' asked Madam-Put-More distractedly. Etuna had come to make change for a departing customer and she was busily calculating the appropriate balance.

'To be the first man to visit every town in the world?'

'Yes,' said Madam-Put-More closing her bag and turning back to her guest. It was not every day she had such an interesting patron. She crossed her attractive legs. 'I'm listening.'

The Stranger paused to convey a delectable chunk of stockfish dripping with well-seasoned egusi soup into his mouth. 'Has my Mercedes passed yet?' he asked Chief Gbedu over his shoulder. There was no little impertinence in his attitude, especially as he had his mouth full of fish. The Chief declined to answer, having decided that the Stranger was rather beneath his status.

'It was in geography class,' he resumed, unperturbed by the snub. 'I counted all the towns in the world on my atlas, you know how many they are?'

'No.'

'Guess. You have to guess or my story is over.'

'Okay, fifty-thousand.'

The Stranger's anger blazed without warning. 'Fifty-thousand! Did I ask how many stars are in the sky? Fifty-thousand indeed! No, not only fifty-thousand, fifty-thousand-million!'

I think it was at that point that Madam-Put-More realised that her patron was, to put it mildly, more than merely interesting. She immediately resolved to end the conversation, but the Stranger cooled off as unexpectedly as he had blown up. 'There are twenty-one-thousand, five-hundred and eighty towns in this world,' he declared with the solemnity of revelation.

He looked around, assuring himself of a wider audience than Madam-Put-More, who was now affecting a greater interest in her money bag. 'With so many towns in this world, it's such a waste of a life not to see them all. So I figured that if I have sixty years before I retire, that gives me twenty-one-thousand, nine-hundred travelling days!' He paused triumphantly, but Madam-Put-More's customers didn't look like they were about to applaud his arithmetic.

The proprietress was studiously totting up the money in her bag; but by this time, the Stranger needed no encouragement. 'So you see, if I spend one day in every town in the world I'll see the whole world before I die!'

'What if you fall sick?' asked Tamara, who never made conversation with customers. 'Or oversleep, or something?'

'I've got three-hundred-and-twenty extra days,' he assured her. 'That's enough for many sick leaves.'

He finished his six wraps of pounded yam with its impressively furnished egusi. An impoverished-looking bus conductor entered and sat beside the Stranger, staring at his incredible table with no little envy. The yellow Mercedes had still not come. The Stranger rose, rinsed his hands thoroughly and walked out to the open-air section. From, there he looked up and down the street, wondering aloud what had become of his friend. Perhaps a flat tyre, he speculated, perhaps their dodgy radiator finally went bust. At the entrance, he paused to sniff again, as though he was receiving more spiritual clues of the town's ancestry. But his eyes fell on the second tray of food and he lurched into his companion's seat and embarked with gusto upon the second meal.

That was when everyone in the restaurant really sat up and paid attention. Someone offered a bet that he could not get beyond the second wrap of amala. It was snapped up.

He promptly lost.

The Stranger's pace was now slower. It seemed as though he had taken the edge off his hunger and was now diligently putting away some more provision for his journey. As he ate, he held forth on his mission.

'I only started out two years ago you know, and already I've done over five-hundred towns.'

Somebody who was quick with numbers figured that out and yelled, 'Hey Stranger, in two years you should have covered seven-hundred-and-thirty towns if you plan to see the whole world before you die!'

'That's all right,' he shrugged manfully, skilfully breaking the treacherous strands of okra that linked his mouth to the plate of drawsoup. 'I've got enough extra days.'

Tamara served the thin-lipped bus-conductor. He had ordered two lonely wraps of eba in oha soup. He could afford neither meat nor fish and the unavailing saliva he was swallowing was provoked by the Stranger's meal. As Tamara poured him a glass of water he muttered confidentially that the Stranger looked powerfully like a bus-conductor he knew very well, who lived and worked at Nnewi motor park. By virtue of his occupation, the conductor's voice was heard throughout the restaurant and the Stranger turned slowly, suspending his amala for the moment.

'I don't like to boast,' he boasted quietly, 'but I don't have much time for this country anymore. Already I have finished the hundreds of villages between Kumaganum and Kaltungo. Dadiya? Done that. Do you know Numan? I've been there. I've travelled to Yola and Ribadu and Girei. It's only Shendam I didn't enter, because of the dysentry there at that time. Have you heard of Eha Amufu? I've been there. I have visited Igumale and Opi. I even got drunk on akpeteshi at a chieftaincy ceremony in Uguta. I've done Okwoga, I've done Oturkpo, I've done Boju. But if there's one town I haven't yet seen, it's Nnewi.'

'Maybe I was mistaken,' offered the intimidated conductor, embarrassed by the attention the Stranger had drawn to the disgraceful meal in front of him.

The Stranger returned to his own meal, mollified. Soon he was tearing at the last chunk of chicken on the plate. There was spontaneous applause when he was done and many patrons queued up to shake his hand. 'That's ok,' he said modestly enough, indicating the slick of soup left on his plate, 'I wasn't really hungry today.'

Well, he rinsed his hands and sat there, a little dazed, but looking rather smug, until Tamara walked up with the bill in her hand. He hesitated and asked uncertainly, 'Did I eat the stewed crab?'

'You didn't order the stewed crab,' Tamara protested.

'My mistake,' apologised the Stranger. Another round of bets were offered, but there were no takers this time. Thirty minutes later, the last limb of the crab had been cracked and sucked dry. Once again, Tamara stood before the Stranger with her bill. 'Tell your Madam to bring it herself,' he instructed her with unmatchable aplomb.

The request bemused Madam-Put-More, but she complied nonetheless. It was her sixth year of running a restaurant and already she had learnt that since there were more buffoons than wise men in the world, to run a successful business she had to humour a lot of idiots.

When she was standing with the bill before the Stranger, he picked up a toothpick and in between picking his teeth and spitting on the table, delivered the following speech.

'I asked you to come so that I could bless you personally. Have I eaten better food in all my life? Hm! Perhaps it was in Nike — or was it Ogoja — that one witch almost approached the consistency of your egusi. Yet, concerning your pounded yam, forget it. It is absolutely matchless. The smoothness and consistency of your yam cannot be compared with my best memories of Ankpa. And as for your drawsoup...' Madam-Put-More's patrons could see a tremor run through him as he took a deep breath. '...suffice it to say, Madam, that you have cooked your way into my dreams.'

Madam-Put-More shook her head self-effacingly and crossed her arms over her bosom; but she was beaming helplessly in spite of herself.

'Now, concerning this bill that your pretty waitress has written,' he continued, burping luxuriantly, 'I am afraid that because of my pressing international mission which — as you rightly observed — leaves a man no opportunity to work, I have no money. You'll have to beat me to your satisfaction.'

'You say what?' demanded Madam-Put-More incredulously, dropping her hands to her waist. The patrons in the open-air section sensed excitement in the offing and they hurried in, clutching their drinks and — for those with food worth stealing — their plates of soup.

'I said you'll have to beat me, that's what I said,' he repeated a little impatiently.

'What about your Rastafarian friend in the yellow Mercedes?' asked Tamara, completely astounded by the turn of events.

A lop-sided grin appeared on his face, like a boy caught out on a prank. 'He's been standing me up from Hadeija to Mberubu; I doubt he will make it today.' He shrugged bravely. 'Let them beat me. A man with a mission has to make personal sacrifices and the pain of weekly beatings is my own cross. — And let me tell you plainly,' he warned sternly, 'I cannot work. I won't do your dishes or any silly nonsense like that. Your only option is to beat me to your satisfaction just as I ate to my satisfaction.' He belched and rubbed his stomach.

Nevertheless, the good people of Ebene would not believe their ears. It was only when he finally shrugged and slung his bag in preparation for departure that it dawned on them that they had indeed shared company with the most outrageous thief. The men with whom he had been joking most evening then moved in on him, cracking their knuckles and loosening their belts from their waists.

That was when he pulled off his shirt to display his rippling deltoid and pectoralis major. At first the vigilantes paused warily, but it was only a cooperative gesture to facilitate a flogging. He laid his shirt down on the table and addressed the enforcers. 'Now you be careful how you beat me, okay? I don't want any mark on any other scar. This very one, this broken weal that is scabbing nicely, this is the mark I got from a fish pepper-soup joint at Lokoja. And this long one is the dagger from an itinerant suya seller at Kotonkarfi.' He hissed with feeling, 'Wretched suya, kept me purging for days.' He arched his back towards his lynch mob, 'Whatever you do, don't touch this black patch on my shoulder. I'm particularly proud of it, got it from an irate buka woman at Nassarawa. She personally poured the hot pap she was drinking on me. Aha, and avoid my head: in Funtua one murderer used a bicycle chain on my head and I started convulsing. Poor idiots. I vomited three plates of peppery jollof rice all over them.' Carefully, he removed a gaudy gold chain from his neck and displayed it proudly before laying it on his shirt. 'One madam in Malumfashi refused to beat me,' he explained, 'she awarded me this gold medal for eating — right from her own neck!'

With that, the Stranger waited patiently to take his medicine like a man.

That was when things started to go horribly wrong. I suppose that something about the Stranger's pompous demeanour rubbed Madam-Put-More the wrong way. If you ask me, I don't know why a thirty-eight-year old spinster shouldn't leave the beating of a thieving vagrant to menfolk, but there you are: what will go wrong will go wrong. What she told the Mother Superior later was: she asked herself just what she was getting out of this. Some thief steals more food from her than a human being can eat; some wife-beaters get some practice slinging punches at a swaying target; — and she carries the deficit. She figured that this sort of thing could catch on easily — and was very bad for business. The Ebene youths could take it in turns to eat large meals and then get slapped around playfully. And how was she then to pay for her meat at the butchers? Was she to barter a beating as well, or a fillet of her laps or what?

Thus, before the Stranger had taken more than five or six slaps and belt strokes on the back, before any mark had actually been inflicted on his body, Madam-Put-More stopped the lynching. 'But we haven't even started,' complained the man who thought he recognised the Stranger at Nnewi. He had just come in from fetching a plank for the beating of the food thief.

'What's it to me if you kill him?' demanded Madam-Put-More, who had hit on an idea to actually make a profit on her food. 'Behind my kitchen is a stack of logs, it will cost me a labourer's wage to make firewood of them. Get him to split them and I would have got my money's worth from him.'

'There's no dignity there,' explained the Stranger with the patience of a teacher of mentally-challenged pupils. 'I never work for my food, just beat me. I've feasted from Gashua to Gwi, from Birnin Kudu to Biu and I've never lifted a hoe. I'm not going to start here.'

The Stranger had apparently never met a woman as conscious of her balance-sheet as Madam-Put-More. 'You can put down your cross, mister man,' she told him briskly. 'You're getting no flogging here. From the size of your mouth, I can see that you've developed the skin of your father, the crocodile. The only punishment you'll get from this town is six months in jail. As I figure it, that's the better part of your extra days down the drain — or 180 towns you'll never see before you die. So just make your choice, young man, between your dignity and your silly mission.'

The Stranger was beaten.

He chose to split the firewood over a stint in detention, slinking with the axe to the backyard like a whipped cur. His very meekness should have warned Madam-Put-More, but she thought she had his measure already. Soon he was splitting wood like any common labourer. Gone was the self-assurance with which he awaited his expected punishment. The marks from Madam-Put-More's restaurant, which in his eyes held no dignity, were the blisters on his tender palms that were not habituated to hard work.

That very night, in a perverted search for his lost dignity, he broke open Madam-Put-More's door with her axe. Taking advantage of a certain silence in Heaven, he took advantage of her with the selfsame axe in his hand. He was gone in the morning and the broken door was a detail she easily explained away. Above everything, she was a practical person. The thing with the Stranger was not a good thing to get around, in the interest of her reputation, and her business.

So despite the pain and the hurt and the hatred inside her, like so many, many women with that sort of secret behind them, she stumbled on through her morning and the middle of her life, until it became impossible to hide the wounding or the festering of the sore, and she turned her restaurant over to a suspicious Tamara, travelling three hundred kilometres to take a long retreat with the Sisters of Mercy at the famous Odozi Convent.

The first time she held the baby in her hand she knew it could never work. She knew that there was an unforgivable passion of hatred for the father of the child, which would always interfere with the love supposed to exist for the fruit of her womb.

In those circumstances, her breasts quickly ran dry. She returned to her business and her balance-sheet, leaving the Stranger in her past and his son to his future in Odozi.

Ψ

The attention in the room shifted from the storyteller to the subject of the story and Somto silently returned the suddenly worried gaze of his foster mother. He even managed a smile as he tried to think nothing, to say nothing, knowing that the turmoil inside him could only get better. He only had to endure until the fever of shock and unutterable grief wore off. He let his head come down slowly until he was face down on Ma'Kanu's bed. He was thirty-six years old, almost at the age his mother was raped, but when he started weeping, he wept like any other rejected child. The sound of him was wrenching to hear.

Ezinne's voice was hard. Why did you tell him, Ma? He didn't need to know, ever.

He wanted to.

Njide sighed despairingly. There was emptiness where there should have been peace, horror where there should have been joy. She said softly, But not like this, Ma. Why did you tell him? You yourself said: no sadness; you yourself said: no tears.

Ma'Kanu's hand trembled on Somto's head and her voice quavered and broke. Didn't you see his eyes when he looked at me? As if I was a witch because there were things too deep for me to forgive?

She was panting. Above her head, Ezinne was busy sign-talking to a wide-eyed Tobe who would otherwise have lost some of Ma'Kanu's tale. Maybe I shouldn't have told you son, maybe it was selfish of me, but I needed you to understand. There are sins beyond forgiveness... You know what your mother said to the nun? She said she hated your father so much she wanted to learn witchcraft just so she could afflict him all his life, anywhere he was. She was ready to be damned to ensure *he* was damned.

Somto looked up. His eyes were bloodshot and mean. This tale, how does it explain why you'll never forgive Kanu and Udeme?

Look me in the eye, SomtoChukwu, tell me you bear no grudge against your father for raping your mother, and your mother for abandoning you ... Ma'Kanu broke off, disconcerted by the look in Somto's eye.

Somto laughed mirthlessly. If only you knew! I want to see them right now! You! You're the one I can't look in the eye!

A sheen of sweat appeared on Ma'Kanu's face. Me? What did I do? All I did was love you all your life!

Love? Do you *understand* love, Ma? How can I love a woman I don't even know. Who *are* you? Where do you come from? You took away our roots, and you couldn't even give us yours!

Somto, began Njide,

No, Sis, she's got to know! My past may be terrible, but I'd rather know it. What other secrets does she have lurking in *her* past? What nasty surprises are we going to discover when she's gone?

Ma'Kanu murmured, All I did... was tell a tale, a true tale in which I played no part.

Like a talebearer, he said bitterly, twisting the barb in my wound to score your point. You had a lifetime to tell me, but you chose your moment, didn't you? Just listen to yourself, preaching your hypocrisy to Igwe Nza! He pushed her trembling hands away and rose. Keep your blessings! he said, stalking away, You need them more than me!

The Saint, urged Ezinne, desperately.

Don't call me that! retorted Somto, snapping away the restraint his nickname had exerted all his life.

Tobe blocked the doorway. His countenance was grave and heavy. His hands flew earnestly: Remember, she promised to listen to you, to forgive Udeme and Kalu, if you were still preaching forgiveness when her tale was done! Preach it!

Well, signed Somto angrily, she can hate all she wants! He turned for the other door. His back had been towards the bed and his response was lost on the others. What did he say? asked Ezinne anxiously, and Tobe's leaden fingers echoed Somto's last words.

As Somto clumped down the veranda steps, Ma'Kanu fell back on her bed, her eyes rolling in their sockets. Ezinne's frightened fingers were frozen in her last question. Tobe clapped explosively and the sound seemed to galvanise Njide. She called out to Somto as she hurried to the new door. By the time she gained the veran-dah, Somto was fumbling the key into the ignition. She cut across the flowerbeds, wincing as tender stems crunched under her feet, thinking that she was too old and overweight for that sort of excitment, and reaching the jeep just as it fired into life. So how can I love you either, she gasped, breathing heavily, since you hid your marriage from us until Getty died?

The engine stopped revving as Njide's words hit home.

Kalu knew! he protested, Udeme knew!

Because you all happened to live in the same town!

Somto clenched his teeth as he tried to hang on to his self-right-eous anger. Guess whose fault that was, he said bitterly. Guess who split us up over Kalu and Udeme's thing...

That's history! said Njide urgently, You have an opportunity to heal the family now. She said she'll listen if you preached forgive-ness now. It's all in your hands, Somto, preach it!

He shut his eyes and bounced his head on the fraying leather of the steering wheel. *Silence in Heaven* overwhelmed him with a paralysing sense of shame and self-hate. The self-image he'd built over four decades was in shreds. He wanted to distance himself from this disgrace, to assuage his own pain by lashing out and *hurting;* his parents were out of the frame, that left Ma'Kanu... He clenched his teeth, determined not to cry, as he shook his head and slammed the gear lever forward. I'm sorry Njide, *I can't.*

Njide stepped back as the jeep pulled away. She picked her way back to the veranda, where she stood bolted, with a handful of mus-lin in her hand, till the roar of the broken muffler faded into silence.

When Njide stepped shakily into the room Tobe was no longer standing there. A sorry breeze lifted the muslin to billow placat-ingly over her head. Ezinne was bent over Ma'Kanu, tepid-spong-ing anxiously. Njide walked woodenly across and laid her hand on the old woman's temple. She snatched it away immediately. She pushed away her sister, lifted the old woman up and stripped away her blouse. She dipped the entire towel into the water bowl and quickly began to rub her down.

Ma'Kanu moaned, eyes still shut. Let me die.

Quiet now, scolded Ezinne, crossing the room to push the win-dows wide open, you've talked enough. This is what comes of blab-bing when you're supposed to be lying-in-state.

Thirty minutes passed and the fever peaked. She lay silently, her eyes staring vacantly at the brown ceiling board that was the entrance to the capacious attic. The younger women sat exhausted on the bed, arms aching, hearts pounding. There was no sound of Tobe, or his anger; the silence worried them more than the distant felling of trees. There was no sound of Somto's jeep either. All they could hear, with the ears of their minds, were the racing tyres of Kanu's car bringing the crux of the problem home from New Bussa.

Suddenly Ezinne started, realising that Ma'Kanu had spoken. She touched Njide who had drifted off and they leaned closer to the old woman. He's always hated me, she whispered, he even kept his marriage secret from me.

Ezinne smiled and shook her head. He hid it from all of us. You know what I think? He was probably embarrassed by his wife!

She did not smile. Her fingers reached out, their nails discoloured and flaking, and seized her daughters' braids. Do you hate me as well? she asked intensely, her eyes rheumy and large. Are you here out of pity — or duty?

The younger women exchanged glances. Njide closed her eyes and she became sixteen years old again, the oldest and, they said, the prettiest of the girls of Orphan House. Her beauty attracted unwanted attention that Christmas when Orachonsi came calling with his suspect auguries. Orachonsi was the lecherous priest of the Afa oracle, which had a penchant for selecting the most beautiful girls as shrine priestesses to serve in the shrine of the idol — and in the bed of its chief priest.

Ma'Kanu had hissed when the 'prophecy' first came to her ears. Toothless old goat with gums good only for the bark of rotting trees, she had laughed, sending off her worried foster daughter to school just as usual. No one else was laughing. The sad case of Nma was still fresh in the villagers' memory, a girl who had also been fingered for shrine work, and who, as the story went, ran mad within a fortnight of rejecting Afa. She had 'jumped' into a well on a conveniently dark night.

Of course some girls had been chosen who had neither run amok nor served Afa's shrine. They had happened to be daughters of men of some means who had deflected Orachonsi's attentions with particularly propitious gifts.

Such gifts were beyond Ma'Kanu's means, were she disposed to make them — which she emphatically wasn't. All the prophecy did was put more fervour into the nightly fellowships she held with her children at Grace Lodge. That night, following the veranda tales and the living-room prayers, as the children and villagers slept, Ma took her torch and silently selected a vicious machete from the trunk. You have to marry the mother with the daughter, she was muttering to herself as she slipped out of her house and left for Afa's shrine.

The shrine was a terrifying grove located a full kilometre from Odozi's borders. A straggling hedge defined the perimeter of the idol's residence, although it claimed the whole of Odozi as domain. A restless baboon paced a bamboo cage by the entrance to the shrine. Orachonsi claimed it held Afa's divining and guardian spirit. It paused in the middle of its circuit and bared its white fangs at the light from Ma'Kanu's torch. The woman leveraged her weapon into the edge of the cage and cracked it open. Then she swung her machete at a recalcitrant thong. She stepped back and made faces and machete swings at the animal that emerged, but the baboon displayed no spirit of guardianship concerning the shrine and disappeared promptly into the darkness.

The most dramatic presence in the enclosure was a fifteen-foot ebony totem the diameter of a small Michelin. If legend could be believed, it had sprouted overnight at that very spot, on the night it adopted Odozi as its domain and Orachonsi as its priest. A hideous one-eyed mask glared down from the very top of the totem. Several other masks, etched with mystic symbols, were carved down the length of the totem. They were spattered with the blood of scores of cockerels and scowled in every direction of the compass.

The shrine of the Afa oracle itself was empty, for it was beyond comprehension that anyone would come to a juju shrine with larceny on his mind; — and Orachonsi for one preferred to sleep in his better-appointed lodgings in the village. The Afa oracle needed no better security than the legend that any mere mortal that touched the totem was sure to run amok.

Ma'Kanu had thought merely to burn it down, not being endowed for tree-cutting. But when she kicked away the sacrificial pots and beamed her torchlight at the base of the totem, she saw that termites — which clearly had no respect for divinity — had already done most of the work. She decided to give them a hand.

Blind scarecrow! she muttered, deploying her machete, feeling a little like Gideon going at his father's idol at night, as she hacked down Odozi's oracle in five angry swings of the machete. You should have kept your cowrie-eye away from my daughter!

Afa's totem crashed into its shrine, breaking handily into four pieces as it fell. Ma'Kanu dragged all the pieces into the raffia shrine, wrinkling her nose at the putrid odour of the entrails in the sacrificial dishes, energized by a passion of fury. She produced a small bottle from her heaving bosom. The decapitated heads of the idol glared at her impotently as she sprinkled kerosene over them. The oracle and its shrine were burning furiously as she turned for home.

When the scandal broke the next morning she maintained a studied silence, making her only comment in the evening at Bacha Line. Right in the middle of central market and in the hearing of Odozi's most respected gossips, she declared that it was impotence, and not just the high bride price that kept statues from marrying wives like other men.

No one needed an oracle to interpret her proverb.

An African oracle could survive any order of gossip touching on its cruelty, its vindictiveness or the inaccuracy of its bolts of thunder. However, it had no defence against ridicule. Orachonsi disappeared within days, although months afterwards another overnight sprouting of a wooden totem was reported in the faraway thickets of Abiagha. Nevertheless, Njide had never forgotten the day Ma'Kanu staked her life and sanity for her foster daughter's future.

Njide would never forget.

She replied softly, You're the silly one, not us, Ma'Kanu. You mothered us for thirty years, what are you going to do or say tonight to make us stop loving you?

But SomtoChukwu...

Njide was silent awhile. If you told me what you told Somto, I'd be hurting too. Remember the day you told us how a long distance bus missed the hairpin bend near Odozi Junction and tumbled down Milken Hill. How it burst into flames, scattering corpses, luggage and debris hundreds of metres down the mountainside. How they found an unconscious baby bleeding in a mango tree, the only survivor of the anonymous bus, whose wreckage lies there till today... How you took the baby home, nursed her back to health and called her Njideka.

She bowed her head. I cried for weeks Ma'Kanu, and I'm still weeping. And there's a wound inside me that will never heal, anytime I think of the man and woman in that bus who gave birth to me.

She brushed her cheeks and raised her eyes to Ma'Kanu. Her voice was firm. I've given up trying to make you out a saint, Ma;

I love you the way you are. I only pray you can release Kanu and Udeme. My real parents may have burnt here; you mustn't burn hereafter.

They felt her body stiffen under them as she released them. They did not rise, and under the very intensity of their eyes, they felt her go slowly limp again. What do you know about Kanu's father? she asked. She pursed her lips but they continued to twitch.

They stared at her blankly, and chorused: Nothing.

Go on! I know you've been pumping Givemore for decades. What have you prised out of him?

That you wedded in Abakiliki, said Njide breathlessly,

And he threw you out for another woman, said Ezinne,

In spite of your pregnancy,

And you moved to Odozi, gave birth to Kanu,

And never want him mentioned again...

They paused, wide-eyed. Was she going to open another taboo subject that night?

Her voice seemed to sigh from the very depths of her. He didn't tell you that the other woman was a nineteen-year-old girl — at the time? An orphan I raised from the age of nine when our foster mother and five brothers died in a fire lit by... my jealous uncle? My only sister, Postie?

No! They exclaimed softly. No! No!

Yes. Decades passed and I forgave my husband, I forgave my sister. She smiled wanly. Weakly, she began to cough; they raised her and after several minutes, she expectorated a bloody gob of phlegm into a clay bowl of sand. She drank some water and sank back onto her pillows.

After long minutes she continued, even more weakly. When Kanu told me it was Udeme or nobody. I almost died. It brought all the bitterness back. He became my husband telling me again that it was Postie or nobody. When they married, I was back in Abakiliki, going crazy all over again. These were children I raised with my own hands! Growing up to deceive me! To betray me! If I knew he had his father's intemperate blood so totally, I'd have been moved to infanticide at childbirth.

She began to weep, her furrowed face wrinkling even more in the agony of her pain. Don't judge me harshly children, but, *I can't forgive.* Even Jesus wasn't crucified twice in one lifetime.

Time bled. Her grief drained into silence. Just when they thought she had slept she murmured, My ankles are killing me.

I'll balm them, said Njide, trying to rise, but Ma'Kanu's leathery palm constrained her.

Don't worry, they can fall off if they want, I won't be needing them soon... she hesitated; tell me your story instead. Her eyes were childlike with pleading, despite the studied casualness of her words.

Njide was startled. She exchanged glances with her sister.

I've no stories to make you laugh.

I'll never laugh again, anyway.

— And the story words... I can't even remember the story words!

Just tell a tale! said Ma'Kanu impatiently.

The beautiful sound of a clap sounded from the doorway and Tobe was standing there. His clothes had matted on his body and he exuded a strong smell of sweat. His usually immobile face was heavy with emotion. His eyes were those of a sufferer. He was a man who could not see a burden but must pick it up. Yet, for once, his shoulders were slumped.

His family stared at him with anxiety. He was the unknown in the House of Grace. He had come full-grown, adopting Ma'Kanu as a boy that appeared out of nowhere, sevenish, mute as a face in a mirror, sleeping at the gate of the fence for two days before the matriarch's heart melted. Ma'Kanu had brought him in, scrubbed him down and gave him a name and a plate of food.

As a project, Ma'Kanu had taken Tobe extremely seriously. She had taken him to the Enugu Teaching Hospital for auditory tests and assessments. His performance intelligence quotient was above normal. X-rays and scans showed no physical defects either in the larynx or the structure of the inner ears. There was no physical reason why he couldn't hear or speak. Yet, Tobe was inarticulate; and he was bilaterally and profoundly deaf. The audiologist concluded he was beyond the help of hearing aids and there was no prospect of his learning normal speech, despite his inexplicable lip-reading skills.

Ma'Kanu turned to the Missionaries to The Deaf. It was a simple thing to get Tobe admitted in their school as a boarding student, but what Ma'Kanu was asking was more difficult. Eventually, a bemused headmistress consented and came to spend a month's vacation at Grace Lodge. For that month, Ma'Kanu set up a blackboard in the living-room and declared the Great Silence. For thirty days, speech was outlawed in Grace Lodge.

Before the month was up the entire household had developed great empathy for Tobe's condition. Ma'Kanu's family became proficient in sign language. They learned the manual alphabet and the rudiments of finger-spelling. On the day of the missionary's departure, they solemnly exchanged sign-names.

Tobe the Loyal. Yet, two things made him totally unpredictable. A passion of violence; and a passion of love.

His hands rose slowly. Ma'Kanu tensed, but his fingers only pledged: I'll tell a tale.

MISSING PERSON

ψ

No 12 Sambo Crescent, Ikot-Ekpene. Long, new house with face-me-I-face-you rooms. Inside room number six, a handsome, middle-aged man reading a newspaper. Handsome, clean-shaven man lying on a mattress, which was lying on the floor. Impatient knock on the door.

'Who's that?'

A muffled, 'Me.'

'Who is "Me"?'

An angry, 'How will you know who I am unless you open the door?'

Man opened door. Grumbled. 'Essien. One has to be careful, you know how the times are.'

'I know how the times are, and I also know that armed robbers don't rob empty rooms like yours. Listen Amatu; the caretaker wants this form completed today. He's sending his daughter for it later. I'm off to work now.'

Amatu took the form and shut the door. He locked it. He looked at the form and put it on his table. He yawned. He walked to the window and opened it. He drew the drapes aside. Ifiok was washing her clothes by the well so he greeted her. He returned to his mattress, scowling. Rude girl, waiting for an elder to greet her first. He straightened the bedclothes on the mattress. He sat down and resumed his newspaper. He read with interest.

KEROSENE EXPLOSION KILLS THREE IN JOS

A kerosene explosion in Dogon-Dutse, near Jos, killed a mother and her two children at the weekend. The Chairman of the Task Force on Distribution of Petroleum Products, said the family brought in the kerosene from Abuja. He however assured the people of Plateau State that kerosene from Jos depot was very safe and that they should not panic unnecessarily...

Amatu stopped. Dogon-Dutse was a long way from Ikot-Ekpene. And even if it were not, he still would not panic. He had neither family nor kerosene stove. He ate his lunches and dinners in local Mama-Puts. No stove was going to blow up in his face. He turned the page.

Unless it was a hurricane lamp.

He shrugged. He began to read again.

SITUATIONS VACANT.

A leading manufacturing company based in Ibadan with branches all over Nigeria has vacancies for a Marketing Manager and an Administration Manager. Applicants must have a B.Sc. in...

He skipped the box. No more salaries for him. Just a small business. A small corner-shop near Sambo Crescent. Basic stock-in-trade: one bag of beans; one bag of rice; one bag of gari. Staff: one small boy to retail the grains from pans. A little money every blessed day. He began to read again.

OBITUARY.

They have done their worst. With deep sadness but total submission to the will of the Almighty God for a life full of achievements, we announce the murder by assassins of our dearly beloved daughter, granddaughter, goddaughter, stepdaughter, niece, aunt, mother, stepmother...

He dropped the newspaper. He leapt six feet across the room to his electric boiler. He yanked the plug out of the socket. The boiling water stopped spilling. He spooned the egg onto a plate. He buttered bread. He made tea. As he made the tea, he shelled some groundnuts. He spread breakfast on the ground. On the bare ground before him.

A cockroach ventured from his wardrobe towards his plate of bread. A foolish cockroach. He smashed it between the groundnuts and the bread. He ate breakfast, his newspaper open before him. His mouth opened for his buttered bread. His buttered bread paused in his hand. His eyes opened even wider. His mouth stayed open as he read.

MISSING PERSON.

Evaristus Mohamu, an employee of Royal Edike Limited has been declared missing. Mohamu, 38, was said to have left his home in Ajegunle, Lagos on May 9 for his office at Tin Can Island and has not been seen since. Fluent in English and his native Tiv language, Mohamu, who is a native of Benue State, is 5 feet 11 inches and dark in complexion. Any information concerning his whereabouts should be sent to his wife, Nkiru Mohamu, through the Editor, or to the nearest police station. Royal

Edike Limited is offering a handsome reward for any useful information.

Amatu began to tremble.

He knew that man!

He put down the buttered slice of bread. He rose and walked to the window. Ifiok had suds up to her elbows. She was singing as furiously as she was washing, her eyes firmly averted from Amatu's window. He turned away. Why did females suppose that every greeting was a precursor to a proposition. He walked to the door. Since May 9. Evaristus had been missing ten months already. He walked to the window again. Slowly he opened the newspaper and stared.

They had chosen a sad picture. A fierce picture too. Handlebar moustache and admiral's beard. Yet, the eyes were naked. The eyes were naked and sad.

Nkiru would be sad too. Naked and sad. Especially with those unpaid bills. Those mounting bills.

Nkiru might be happy though. Naked and happy. Especially with the coast clear now. Especially with the stammering Edike there.

He sat down on the mattress. Evaristus Mohamu a missing person! What a way to go! He stretched out his legs. The egg was cold. The tea was very cold. He ate the egg. He drank the cold tea down.

Chief Royal Edike would be cold too. Edike would be cold with rage. Likely, still stocktaking his huge warehouse...

He knew that family well! He had never pitied a human being the way he pitied poor Evaristus. Often he had called Nkiru to one side. Often he had talked to her: This was no way to treat her husband, he'd said. Many people were interested in that marriage as well. Chief Royal Edike also called her aside as well, and talked to her...

Then she got pregnant. At last, after trying and trying, finally she got pregnant. The boy came. Amatu had never seen a baby so full of itself. Lying there in the middle of countless shouting matches, sucking its toes and fingers and bubbling with joy. Yet, in the end, that joy seemed to infect the marriage. Days would pass without a quarrel. A whole week without a fight. Three years did pass. As the boy toddled and grew, it seemed that the marriage would also toddle and grow.

Then he started to stammer. A three-year-old boy with a bad stammer.

Like Chief Royal Edike's bad stammer.

Amatu ate a slice of buttered bread. Missing Person! What a way for a sales clerk to end up. He ate another slice of buttered bread. He had buttered it so absently that it was more like breaded butter. He frowned. Was it the butter? Was it the bread? Was it his old pity for poor Evaristus? He pushed away his plates. Would the police ever find him? Or would they one day find a corpse? A ritually murdered corpse desecrated and mutilated beyond recognition... File closed?

Amatu folded the newspaper and stretched out on the mattress. He shut his eyes. He reminisced; slowly, he drifted off.

Timid knock on door. Amatu started, scaring two enterprising cock-roaches from his last slice of bread. He yelled. 'Who is that again!'

A shy voice. 'Idiong, the caretaker's daughter.' Amatu rose reluctant-ly. He sat at table and pulled up the tenancy form. He took a pen. Quickly he filled out name. And age. And occupation. Then he paused. He sighed deeply. He tore the form. He walked to the door and opened it.

The caretaker's daughter stood there. Thirteen years old and grow-ing fast. Her hand was open and waiting. 'Tell your daddy I made a mistake,' he said, 'I need another form.' She nodded and walked down the corridor to the next room. She was wearing her braids in a tortoise-shell clasp.

He slammed the door shut. His mirror hung on a nail on the door. It rattled dangerously. He turned the key. He stared at his sad eyes, which stared back at him, naked and sad, hunting for a doorway back into the past. They grew sadder as he recalled the face of the three-year-old boy who had called him 'Paaaaaapa!'. The little boy who could only fall asleep on his chest with a thumb in his mouth and one tiny hand lost in the hairs on his chest. Who would not know why he stammered. Who would have waited many lonely evenings at the door of those lonely rooms at Ajegunle, for Paaaaaapa! to come back. Who would not un-derstand the politics, and the bitterness, and the complexities of grown-ups. Amatu touched his painful razor bumps.

Sometimes it was not so easy to make Evaristus Mohamu disappear.

Ψ

They began to clap as Tobe's hands fell to his side. He raised his hands again and asked, You liked it? I hadn't finished: I was just resting my hands! So they clapped some more. Modestly he turned away. Soon they heard him in the bathroom scooping water from the vat into a bucket. Presently they heard the sound of bathing.

The peace in the living-room was breached by a gunshot from Ikpe Quarters; but the silence that reclaimed the night was even more profound than the one before the gunshot. Ezinne looked at the clock on the wall. It was almost 3 am! Kanu and Udeme did not make it after all. Perhaps it was for the better.

Did you see TobeOlisa? whispered Ma'Kanu proudly, Did you see the drama in his body, how he silently took us to that terrible room in Ikot-Ekpene?

First story he ever told, mused Ezinne.

I bless God I lived to hear it, said Ma'Kanu. I bless the Lord for the day I conquered my prejudice and opened my door for a deaf-mute street kid who adopted me himself.

Njide looked at the door to the old Boys Room through which Tobe had disappeared. It's the saddest story I ever heard, she said in a very small voice. That poor boy waiting for his father... reminds me of Tobe himself. He's the strongest of us, yet, sometimes, you see in his face ... that lack of understanding of a complicated world...

Amatu himself cuts a sadder picture, mused Ezinne, the boy will wait for his father for a week or two. The man will be looking back to his son forever.

A silly man if I ever saw one, said Ma'Kanu indignantly, The boy called him 'Pa' for goodness sake! Nothing else mattered!

There was a significant pause and when it stretched too long, Ma'Kanu shrugged and asserted, with some discomfiture: The boy was three years old for goodness sake! Nothing was his fault!

Grace Lodge grew more silent as Tobe moved from bathroom to bedroom. They listened to him dress. There was a strange peace in him as he strode out, buttoning his sleeves. In his shirt pocket was the notepad and pencil he used in communicating with people illiterate in sign. His bag was slung on a shoulder.

Ma'Kanu was alarmed. Where are you going?

Depends on you, he replied, coming to her bedside. When my mother led me to your gate that night, twenty-seven years ago, she told me you were the greatest mother in the world. — If you would only accept me.

There was an incredulous silence in the room. It was the silence of deafness, the silence of mutism, the silence of dead places. Ma'Kanu whispered, her fingers articulating numbly, Your mother? *Your mother?* You always said you didn't remember anything; that you found yourself at the scene of an accident and started walking...

I lied. My mother warned me to. She *underlined* her last note to me. He sat by the foot of the bed, facing the three women. Quietly, in sure movements, he fished out the notepad. He put it on his lap. His hands lifted, trembled and were still. They began to speak surely: My mother was demented. She had her lucid intervals, but she was mad — I'll never forget her.

Who is she? asked three anxious sets of hands. *Where* is she?

He took the pencil from his pocket and poised it over the pad. Then he replaced it and instead, began to sign spastically. I remember the day I lost my hearing. And my speech. That was the day my fathers died.

Your fathers?

Remember the story I just told? Well, *I* was the stammering toddler. Only the names and towns were fiction. Amatu was my father — and after three or so years, he walked into our new house. By then my mother had remarried my new father. They had the longest quarrel in the world, all three of them, while I stood there watching. Amatu said he came back for me... but *I didn't remember him*... it was all my fault, what happened next...

What happened? demanded Njide.

I called Royal 'Pa'. My father went ballistic. He attacked Royal with a kitchen knife. I saw it go in once, twice, thrice... My mother fainted. I just stood there, staring, until Amatu came to me. He held me with the dry hand, the hand that had no blood. He told me to call *him* 'Papa' — and to be sure not to stammer. I opened my mouth. I was looking at the hand with the blood, at the hand with the knife. I tried to say 'Papa'. To say it without a stammer...

Tobe paused. I think that was when I lost my voice, he finished.

But his trembling hands garbled his sign language. What? asked Ezinne.

I haven't said a word since then, confessed Tobe silently.

Ezinne's fingers cramped into claws. She had tears in her eyes. Was that when you also lost your hearing? she mouthed.

Tobe stared intently as he penetrated a three-decade-old memory. No. I remember the gurgling from Royal's lungs as he died. I remember Amatu yelling at me to call him 'Papa'. My hearing died later, with Amatu... I heard his first scream, then everything went silent. His mouth was still opening and closing, the blood was spouting from his throat, but I never heard anything anymore.

How did he die? Asked Njide.

My mother recovered from her faint and saw him bent over me with a knife. She broke a chair on his head. He dropped the knife and fell on top of me. He was very strong. He rose and turned to her. He fell on top of her. He was strangling her. I picked up the knife from beside me. I stabbed him once. In the neck. I was seven.

You killed Amatu? whispered Ma'Kanu.

That wasn't his real name, of course, said Tobe. There was a lot of madness in the air that day. My mother kept us there. With her decomposing husbands. Till the smell forced the neighbours to break in. That was when we became vagrants, how I became a street kid...

His composure finally cracked. He hid his face in his hands for a long moment. When he had gathered himself, he began to speak again. My mother knew where to find you. You'd done your teaching-practice here and fallen in love with the hillside. In her lucid moments, the thought of me was all that kept her from suicide... she'd be dead now...

He broke off to collect himself. ... Then I met you. I was an old man in a boy's body when I met you, but you... made me young again. By the time I learnt how to fingerspeak, I *knew* you... and I was too afraid to lose your love to tell you the truth. Yet, after tonight I can see that everything built on deception will eventually fail. We have lived a lie, but we must not die in it. This is my mother's name, He picked up his pencil, scribbled a name on a page and, tearing it off, held it out to her with a steady hand.

Ma'Kanu's eyes didn't leave his own. The hand she extended trembled. As her fingers touched the paper, Tobe saw the alien set of her jaw and his nerve broke. He snatched back the sheet and ripped it into shreds. Grunting in despair, he splintered his pencil like a stalk of spaghetti, flinging the pieces and fragments away from him.

He clasped his hands over his face for the three minutes it took him to gather himself. When he looked up, Ma'Kanu was looking at him with a steady, implacable gaze. Soberly, with a joyless smile, he raised his right hand. He made a fist, bent it over, and extended his index finger before his middle finger.

P, spelt Ezinne hoarsely.

Tobe opened a fist halfway and touched his index finger with his thumb.

O, spelt Njide tersely.

He folded his fingers at the second knuckle and crossed his index and middle fingers with his thumb.

S, whispered Ezinne.

When Tobe, with agonizing precision, clenched a soft fist and pushed his thumb between index and middle fingers, Ma'Kanu lifted herself from the bed and screamed, shattering the pre-dawn quiet. *POSTIEEEEE!*

The new peace of Tobe's countenance was unscratched. Without losing his smile, he dropped to his knees, his hands rising in supplicative speech. I know what she did to you. Forgive her now, Ma. We're your blood. We've already gone through hell on earth. We've paid. And she spoke of you, loved you every step of the way...

But the old woman only screamed louder and pummelled him with pillows in a new, demonic power. Damn you! Get lost! I never want to see you again!

A new Tobe rose, stowing away his notepad. He didn't fly into a wordless, tree-cutting rage. It seemed a peace of acceptance, a peace that surpassed understanding, had overtaken him. He plucked his last story card from his pocket and dropped it on Ma'Kanu's bosom. Ma'Kanu's hand had written the one word, Regret.

He smiled at a thunderstruck Njide and squeezed Ezinne's frozen shoulder. Ezinne clenched her teeth and her fingers flew: *Amatu, Royal, Postie... none of them was your fault!* Tobe nodded absently, picked up his bag, and walked to the door. As his footsteps faded away and Ma'Kanu sank back into bed, Dada's sleepy voice came over the eastern wall, *Sorryooo!*

Njide fell back on the bed so that she was lying side by side with Ma'Kanu. The old woman might have been dead but for the tinny rasping of her breathing. Ezinne began to sing in a trembling contralto perfectly appointed for the wake of a close relative, raising her voice to drown the sound of Njide's weeping.

O ga som ka'm bulu enyi Jesus
Ka'm bulu enyi Jesus
Ka'm bulu enyi Ya O

An hour passed with the tableau unchanged. Then Njide sat up and blew her nose. When Ezinne had fallen silent she declared, I will tell a story. But Ma'Kanu continued to stare wordlessly at the ceiling.

As she composed herself to begin, an explosive fusillade was released from the direction of Ikpe Quarters. Ezinne looked at her watch. It was just after 4 am. It was the final send-off for Chief Ude, a gunshot for every decade of the septuagenarian's life.

At that moment they heard the sound together. There was no mistaking the broken muffler. Ma'Kanu did not stir but her eyes refocused on the middle distance. They tensed as the sound grew steadily louder, until it paused at the gate of the house.

When the engine of the jeep died, three car doors slammed and the women became conscious of another racket. For a moment they could not fathom it, then it resolved into the sound of quarrelling: voices of grieving and a voice of assurance. Three voices bickering as they approached the bungalow.

You lied! You lied to us!

I tell you she's alive! She's there with the rest.

So what were those gunshots? Who's hunting at 4 am? Come on, we're no kids!

I tell you, that was someone else's burial, Chief Ude's...

They gained the veranda and paused.

What's her bed doing in the living room? demanded Udeme in a ragged whisper, then she screamed as she broke through the veranda and into the house. She was in the middle of the room before she stopped, rooted to the spot. Her wild eyes absorbed the wasted body on the bed and jumped to all the wrong conclusions.

She was short and fair-complexioned, still in the middle of the impulse that sent her headlong through life, ricocheting off the facets of her many-sided ambitions. Her handsome face was still aquiline, but the rest of her body was broadening with a determination that was thoroughly Udeme. Her cheeks were dusty and tear-streaked, ordinarily she was a take-charge personality, but there was not a shred of composure in the woman who stood staring at

Ma'Kanu, afraid to go further. She began to wail in a voice liquid with sorrow, in that unashamed nakedness of one that spoke to a corpse, pouring out her heart without filter and without restraint: No Ma, you're not dead Ma, we didn't embrace first, you didn't bless me first...

Behind her, Kanu stood at the doorway, his cap crushed in a trembling fist, the muslin curtain strangled in the other. He stood, incredibly, taller than his first-cousin Tobe, and just as broad in the shoulders, with a stature his incontinent father had bequeathed him.

But all that stature made his wreck all the more colossal. His sisters drank in the sight of him, for they had not met in a decade; yet, he had eyes only for his mother on the bed. He had spent hours on the deserted highway trying to coax a stuttering carburettor back to life, before Somto stumbled across them. He did not appear to be crying, but his hasty fingers had left grease marks on his cheeks. He was similarly frozen, unable to go forward. His voice was a hoarse croak: Njide, did she ask for us...

Never, came the cold voice from the apparition on the bed. She did not take her eyes from the ceiling as she spoke. Get out of my house, I never want to lay eyes on you, ever.

Udeme gasped and reeled backwards, not believing the venom in the words that issued from the wraith on the bed. The conflict of emotions — relief that she was still alive, and despair at her unrelenting hatred — staggered her. Ezinne hurried to her side and took her in an embrace.

No! cried Kanu from his knees where his mother's brutal words had dropped him. Don't be like this, Ma!

I'll never bless you, said his mother matter-of-factly, and if I don't see your face, I won't curse you either.

At those words, the stone-faced Somto who had remained on the veranda stepped in and lifted Kanu to his feet. Firmly he steered him around and led him back onto the veranda. As he passed the doorway, he unhooked his baseball cap and stuffed it down an orange pocket in a grave and final gesture. Ezinne and Udeme joined them. Let's go, said Somto descending the steps.

However Kanu's hand had laid hold of a post that linked the railings to the eaves, and he was a stubborn man. He had driven a few hundred desperate kilometres behind a stuttering engine and a pause was indicated. Udeme's knees gave way at the topmost step and she sat down heavily. Ezinne sat down beside her, but it was not necessary. The woman from New Bussa was no longer weeping. Instead there was a thin, joyless smile on her face. Fine, she said softly, if that's the way she wants it.

In the living-room Ma'Kanu listened fretfully for the footfalls that would take the cursed children from her house but they did not come. All she heard were Somto's grim footfalls as he picked his way to the jeep. She listened as he uncoupled the towline from the car behind and drove off slowly. On the veranda, Udeme's eyes panned over the wild garden, which lay in the shadows. She said to Ezinne in a small, bitter voice that carried: Tell her I have flowers to die for, in a garden that she'd wish she came to see.

Tell her I don't want to see her garden! shouted Ma'Kanu truculently.

Tell her we found her *dendrobium* three years ago. — And I grew a species more fragrant than she used to know.

Ma Kanu's intake of breath was audible on the veranda.

Tell her, growled Kanu, that we called it the *dendrobium makanus*.

Ezinne told Ma'Kanu nothing. It was not necessary. They listened for her angry riposte. It did not come. When Ma'Kanu's favourite orchid died two decades earlier, it had been impossible to replace because she had not known its true identity in the first place. She had been haunted for years by its subtle nighttime fragrance, a tangy citrus with a hint of peppermint. Udeme rose and walked to the gate, opened the back door of their car and carefully brought out a potted plant. It had been scarfed to protect its dramatic white flowers from the breeze. Udeme stomped into the living room, breathing heavily from the exertion, and unfurled her prize. It was a striking specimen in full bloom. Close to a dozen flowers swayed gently, a dash of reddish orange in their throats. She set the pot down carefully beside the bed. She straightened up, barely a foot from her mother.

Ezinne, said Udeme, staring bitterly at Ma'Kanu whose eyes were shut firmly, tell her that I brought it for her grave, so it's hers to smash up, even now.

With that, Udeme returned to Ezinne's side on the veranda. She slipped her hand into Kanu's. She raised her face into a cool breeze, willing it to penetrate through to the fire in her bosom.

Inside the house, Ma'Kanu opened her eyes and glared at an Njide who was no longer weeping. She was looking at her foster mother with something like pity in her eyes. Ma'Kanu caught the expression, which riled her the more. She had not glanced sideways at the orchid, nor reached towards it — whether in rage or wonder. Yet, to Njide's ears it seemed that the rasping of her mother's breath was deeper, hungrier; as though she would dredge the very air of all its fragrances. You want to leave as well? demanded Ma'Kanu.

Njide said hoarsely. I'll never stop loving you, Ma'Kanu... but you aren't human.

— And I haven't left you, grandmother, called Ezinne with her trademark irreverence, but we have guests, as you can see.

The old woman flinched, but she was too afraid of dying alone to indulge her anger. Her body trembled from the ravages of pain; and from the strain of averting her eyes from the plant next to her. But just then, she was too proud to ask for help. She breathed deeply and turned her pinched face to the ceiling as Njide reached for the tub of liniment. Her daughter softly began to ply her knee joints. The humanity in Ma'Kanu sighed.

After what seemed like an age, her broken voice whispered, humbled by her need. You promised me a tale.

Njide hesitated. I did, she admitted and shut her eyes. She took a deep breath. The ugly present fled her mind and, transported by the exotic fragrance of Udeme's orchid, suddenly she was a teenager again, throwing aside the cares of the day to spin a tale for the night; painting, with the canvas of her words, fantastic scenes that had existed only in her mind. The misery of her reality dropped away and she felt she could fly; Story, story, she called from two decades away; — and opened her eyes onto the present with a start.

Her foster mother was also staring at her, with not a little dismay. Yet, the words were out: nursery words that prepared juveniles for a kindergarten tale. Njide repeated them stubbornly, rather like an automatic teller machine that would only dispense its tale on the satisfactory production of a password.

Story, mumbled Ma'Kanu in a low, embarrassed voice, conscious of the children on the veranda, who were no longer children.

Story, story! demanded Njide mischievously; and sheepishly, the eavesdroppers on the veranda confirmed their interest one after the other. She took a deep breath, her heart bleeding for the deaf-mute stumbling around in the darkness of Odozi — and for the sudden victim of a forty-year old rape, who was driving to and fro in confusion. As the gathered family listened, separated by wooden walls of resentment and unforgiveness, she told her tale.

ZURU JUNCTION

ψ

'I will die an amazing death, praise the Lord!' boomed the voice, 'I will glorify God with my death! After I die, I will be even more famous than the president!' Legris turned from the cut of meat he was haggling over to the sound of the voice. He sneered at the sight. There in the midst of the ram-sellers of Kano's Sabongari Market, was a young man in a dirty-gray caftan flailing a Bible held together with a thick rubber band. In his face was that earnest zeal of the recently-saved. His right hand held a microphone whose loudspeaker was slung on his back.

Nobody paid him much attention but he did not seem deterred. Instead he repeated his words with confidence and aplomb: 'Praise the Lord! I will die an amazing death! I will glorify God with my death! Hundreds of thousands will view my corpse in silence!' Then he turned and picked his way, with uneven steps, over the black cobblestones set in the stream of reddish drain-water that was the path out of the ram section.

'Who is that man?' demanded Legris of the blood-spattered butcher before whose stall he stood.

'A preacher,' replied the butcher without interest, describing a loony circle near his head with a finger. He lifted the shank of ram from his knife-scarred chopping-board with affected effort, as though he were lifting an iron slab. 'Look at what you're pricing in God's name! Just lift it and see! The money you are calling is not money, price this meat well! Even if I cut this from a dead animal in the gutter I can't sell it at that price!'

'The way it is smelling,' said Legris cruelly, 'maybe that's where you cut it from.' He walked away from the stall, ignoring the offended butcher's abuse. It had been a very hot day and at 6 pm he decided it would be difficult to get fresh meat in the local stalls. He turned his feet towards the fish section, deciding to settle for a different sort of dinner that night.

Of course it was not so much that the meat was foul, as that Legris' mood was foul. Over the past few years, his temper had been deteriorating as steadily as his fortunes. Right then, although he had his salary in his hip pocket, it was nothing to cheer about; it was such a thin envelope that he had to spend carefully, even on payday.

Some other butchers had observed his interest in meat and they tried to grab him with their bloodstained hands. He roared at them and they took the hint, leaving him severely alone.

'Is it my fish you are pricing or the eggs in its stomach?' demanded the irritated fishwife whose two-year-old son sucked lustily at one huge breast while her oily right hand paused on the lip of a bowl of tuwo. She had made good sales that day and her very last catfish was in no danger of returning home with her. She was therefore in no mood to humour idiocy. 'Look my friend, if you don't have money for fresh fish go and buy tinned sardines. It is no sin to cook soup without fish.'

Legris glared sourly from the tempting catfish he was bargaining for to the obese fishwife with a fraying straw hat perched on a stool behind her wares. His mouth opened in a caustic reply but just then, a loud-speaker hailed from some fifty metres away. 'Praise God for me! I will die an amazing death! I will glorify God with my death! My corpse will be even more famous than our president's own!'

'For goodness' sake!' snapped Legris angrily. 'Won't a man live a famous life before he dies a famous death? I come to the market for food and all I find is diseased meat and rotting fish and crazy preachers...' He broke off as the fishmonger leapt to her feet, hand dripping soup, her son's mouth disengaging from her breast with an audible plop.

'Thief!' screamed the apoplectic fishwife, 'My fish is rotting and yet he wants to buy it!' She clapped hysterically for attention. 'Look at this useless thief that wants to steal rotting fish! Has this one even eaten fresh fish in five years? Is my boy not more of a man than this one? It's only your mother than I pity, poor woman; bearing you and dancing that she has born a man child!'

The fishwife's unaided voice was even louder than the preacher's. Heads began to turn as shoppers suspended their last-minute shopping to watch what was building up to be an interesting spectacle. Urchins gathered. Legless beggars skidded up on their skates. The muscle-bound market porters in the immediate vicinity left their barrows and drifted over to the scene of the latest excitement. 'Myself?' Legris countered, backing cautiously away from the fishwife's demonstrative limbs, 'I said your fish was rotting? Don't be annoyed now, is it not your body odour that confused me?'

But he was no match for the association of fish sellers who rose as one body and poured a venomous diatribe on him.

'AIEEE!' screamed the corpulent fishwife, diving for Legris' neck. 'You want to kill me because I won't dash you my fish! You will kill me today!'

The half-naked woman, having secured Legris' tie with her food-stained hand, was in the process of garrotting him. In point of fact she would surely have killed Legris that day, with the enthusiastic support of the other fishwives, but for the presence of the more phlegmatic porters who reluctantly prised Legris from their clutches when things began to get out of hand.

A frightened Legris bolted from Sabongari market, reeking of fish and sour kaushe soup and pursued by jeering urchins. His shirttail was flying, one shoe had lost both buckle and strap and his tie would never pass muster again. He looked like someone who had only just survived an argument with a lynch mob. By a miracle, the bottle of groundnuts in his briefcase was not broken. Moreover, he was still hanging on to his nylon bag of foodstuff; although the tomatoes inside would no longer need grinding.

He stopped running about a hundred metres from the market and tried to compose himself. Next to him, a young woman was hawking frozen fish but when he felt in his rear pocket, the envelope containing his wages was gone. His trembling fingers felt through the rest of his pockets and turned up some loose change. Enough for the bus fare back to his room. Enough for a tin of sardines for his dinner, to complement the three hundred grammes of rice, a small onion, five tomatoes and a tiny nylon pouch containing some tablespoons of vegetable oil. Enough for dinner but no assurance of breakfast. After that he could not yet think.

A cold rage began to build in him.

He stumbled back to the bus stop where he stood patiently in line. He was trembling uncontrollably. He shut his eyes and he began to curse. As he waited on the queue he could feel a bladder inside him swelling with venom and he knew that his bile would poison anyone who pricked him at that moment. As he waited for a bus to take him home, a hawker passed by with a tray of provender from which he bought a tin of sardines, growing angrier as he did so.

As he waited for the thirty-three-seat Coaster bus that passed within a five-minute walk from his room, a young man in a cheap polyester caftan limped up to join his queue. He unslung his burden and put it on the ground. Legris felt that the bladder of venom was actually his skull, because he felt so light-headed, he could float. His bitterness focused as he watched the young man's mouth. 'Say it,' he muttered to himself, edging towards the preacher. 'Just say it again.'

The young man's mouth parted in greeting as he conversed with the women at the rear of the queue. It stretched in a smile as he caught

Legris' fixed stare and nodded at him. However, it did not speak the words that so infuriated Legris.

Eventually, a bus arrived and was promptly filled with enthusiastic commuters. Amidst the bustling and confusion of the boarding, little else was clear until Legris found himself two seats behind the preacher. Two stops later, the seat before him fell vacant and Legris moved up without thinking, placing his fingers on the preacher's headrest, each hand an inch from the neck of his tormentor.

The preacher threw back his head and laughed at something the man at his side had said. The bus crawled on.

At Legris' bus-stop close by Zuru Junction, the bus stood wheezing as it waited for three passengers to debark. Legris' room was five minutes away. It was empty. Four years ago his father-in-law had thrown him out, keeping his wife and his two daughters. He had moved into his present quarters where he lived alone ever since.

His miserable dinner — rice, insipid stew and the infuriating sardines — was only thirty minutes away. Yet, it was also the thirty-first day of January and the caretaker's door would be open as usual. No tenant in that house could enter his room without passing that open threshold at the head of the corridor; — and Legris had nothing to put into those merciless, avaricious fingers. The three commuters stepped down and the bus moved on with Legris.

All the meanness and the savagery and the bestiality of Legris' life surged upon him until he felt that he was dying from a blood poisoning induced by bitterness. In that flood came bitter memories of better times when there always were bags of rice and millet in his pantry. Times when his pantry alone was the size of his current lodgings.

He recalled his disastrous investment with the swindler that made away with his trading capital. He recalled how in desperation he had turned the balance of his fortunes to shamans and other prayer swindlers. He saw himself tumbling from his duplex to the three bedroom flat near Gidan Murtala and thence to the studio apartment by Bayero University. He recalled the stint at his father-in-law's house, into which he had been pushed by dire extremity. With wrenching shame, he recalled his disgraceful eviction that Christmas Eve, four years before, after he resolved never to polish his father-in-law's shoes again.

He focused on the preacher's head. He did not know how to get the meanness out of his life. But tonight he had a focus for his rage.

The bus ground to a halt again and six persons got off. About a dozen climbed on and as they did so, the preacher rose to his feet. Immediately, Legris began to rise, only sitting back when he realised that the preacher had risen to yield his seat to a fat woman. The woman sat down with Legris, thanking her benefactor effusively.

The preacher stood with one hand clutching his backpack and the other gripping the frame of the seat he had just vacated. The bus bounced and the preacher's hand touched Legris'. The latter snatched his hands into his laps. The preacher's shorter right leg braced against the seat but his balance was precarious and every time the big bus lurched, which was often, he swung back and forth.

Who's he trying to impress, anyway, fumed Legris silently, standing for a well-fed woman who ought to be standing for a cripple like him.

Presently, the preacher did disembark. Legris let two men descend after him before following, clutching his briefcase and nylon bag.

Night had fallen.

The traffic flowed past like a drift of water hyacinths on a clogged up river. On the roadside, a few pedestrians milled. The preacher limped along towards Zuru Junction. Legris followed hard on his heels, determined not to lose sight of him. The preacher stopped at a seedy electronics shop and checked in his hired public address system. Right outside, he paused by a food hawker whose stall was lit by the flame of a kerosene lamp, he inclined his head and spoke in low tones. Presently, he smiled and sat down, unfastening his Bible.

Fifteen angry minutes later, Legris was still shifting from leg to leg, slapping at the energetic, suicidal mosquitoes that flew sorties at his exposed limbs. By the time the preacher finally moved on, Legris' mood could not be fouler. They walked like that for a dozen feet or so before the preacher turned around and walked the two paces that brought him face to face with Legris. He was smiling but there was some uncertainty in his face as he asked, 'Why are you following me.'

'Your preaching,' said Legris truthfully enough. 'It annoys me and I don't agree with it. Do you mind expatiating on it?'

The smile grew wider. 'Certainly.'

'Not here,' said Legris hastily, as the other man began to tug at his fat rubber band, 'let's go somewhere more quiet,' and without waiting for his assent, he pushed past him. Another three dozen paces and Legris found himself at the Zuru level-crossing. Without turning to see if the preacher would follow, he turned right at the crossing, ducked through a break in the wire and entered the darkness of the fenced-off railway track. A sheer wall rose on the right and ran away from him. Along the wall was a collage of human excrement. He walked several more steps into the deserted track, reassured by the crunching of gravel behind him.

Then he stopped. He was three feet from the railway track and was himself afraid of the deeper darkness beyond. He turned around and, sure enough, there was the boy standing about six feet from him. 'This is quiet enough, now preach.'

'What don't you understand?'

Legris felt a surge of power as he recognised fear in the voice and posture of his companion.

'You said you will be a star when you die,' said Legris circling the boy slowly. 'Show me where it says so in your book.'

The preacher hesitated. 'I am sorry, I don't know what got into me today. I normally don't preach like that, it is not in the book...'

Legris continued to circle, surreptitiously searching his surroundings. There had to be something on the ground that could be a cudgel. Something that could be a weapon. 'So explain it to me,' he said, 'I don't understand.'

The lad was turning on one spot to keep his eyes on Legris. 'Today was different. Today, every time I opened my mouth, I preached about what I was full of. You see, yesterday night... I saw a vision...'

'How is that my business?' demanded Legris, he was getting desperate, there was nothing except the gravel. 'Or the business of any of us at the market? Why should you disturb us with your crazy visions?'

The boy struggled with his thoughts and his words. 'They were visions about my death. In the past, when I dreamt of death, I woke up praying: God forbid! But yester night, for the first time since I became a Christian, I had no fear of it. There was so much light in that death that I saw, it was so glorious... I wanted to die right away...'

'Is that so?' asked Legris, sitting on a rusting post sunk into the ground and cutting off the only exit from the enclosure. His heart began to beat faster as he remembered the bottle of groundnuts in his briefcase. A tap of the bottle on the post he was sitting on would transform it into a weapon of mayhem. His voice became malicious. 'Then why do I see fear in your eyes right now?'

The boy swallowed and took a deep breath. 'Maybe this is my Garden of Gethsemane...'

'No,' growled Legris, 'this is your Zuru Junction.'

He set down the nylon bag and pulled out the bottle of groundnuts from his briefcase. He unscrewed its cap. Because it was not an innocent gesture, what should have been a simple action became very clumsy. Spilling nuts on the gravel, he managed to get some onto his palm and began to eat. 'Have some.'

'Ah... no, thank you.'

Legris ate quietly, trying to determine with his ears if there was any-one within screaming distance. Then it occurred to him that in Kano metropolis people fled from screams that came from the darkness, not towards them. Thus fortified, he asked. 'Did you see me in your vision yesterday?'

'I... don't think so, but what is important is that whatever your prob-lems are, Jesus...'

'Just don't start that,' warned Legris.

'I thought you wanted me to expatiate.'

'Expatiate on how a wretched beggar like you can become a famous corpse. Expatiate on that.'

The boy hugged his book and threw a backward glance into the dense darkness. He shifted his weight up onto his good leg but gravity soon pulled him down onto the bad. 'For a man it is impossible but with God it is a simple thing... Jesus was a wretched corpse too, but he is more famous now than many presidents...'

Legris sneered, 'So now you are Jesus Junior! Do you know what you caused me?' he demanded bitterly. There was a great hopelessness in his life that was growing and growing and he tried to think beyond the moment of his violence with the boy, but he couldn't.

'What?'

'There I was trying to buy meat when you came with your wretched prophecy. — I'm not crazy, you know, I was crazy years ago, but I am not anymore. I'm going to tell you just how it is. — You and your kind have cost me dearly, you know. There I was trying to make a life for myself and you came and messed me up, messed me up, messed up my mind —'

'Me?'

'I said you and your kind! That's what I said! And don't go inter-rupting me, because you're really really getting me angry now, okay? Fine! There I was trying to make a life for myself and another idiot who called himself a preacher came at me, the thief. May he burn in hell! Seeing visions every night was a small thing. He saw them as he walked. Always visions of how my cars became his own. How my bank account augmented his own. Keep your eyes on Jesus, you say and you skinned me, you robbed me, you —'

'Me?'

'Just you shut up, okay,' snapped Legris from his feet. He had taken the bottle by the neck and pointed the base at his tormentor. A stream of nuts trickled to the gravel and stopped as he lowered his hand to continue. He knew now that he was working himself up to do something that he could not do in cold blood. Already his heart was pounding with hate. 'Do you know that I once used to own two houses? Do you know that one of them is now a church and the other a preacher's residence? DO YOU KNOW THAT? Do you know that I cannot pay the rent for my room tonight because of you and your stupid preaching? Do you know that I have a family I have not seen in years because of the robbery you practised on me? Do you know that I have a B.Sc. Accounting that is older than you and yet I am practically a destitute? Do you know that you are a fraud? That everything you are saying is a fraud?'

'No,' said the boy, firmly.

'Yes, you are a fraud,' pronounced Legris taking a step forward, glad for some opposition, any confrontation. 'That book you are holding is a fraud. You are a fraud. Look at you, wretched cripple like you, preaching about miracles. You need a real miracle yourself, but all you are preaching is the miracle of my money entering your pocket! You start out seeing visions of your death. Soon it will be the death of any idiot foolish enough to listen to you, while you inherit his property!'

'This book is not a fraud,' said the boy in a ringing voice, 'I am not a fraud. You may have met some wolves in sheepskin but God is not a fraud.'

'Well, tonight you're going to find out about that!' said Legris swinging the bottle at the post behind him. It connected with a dull crack and groundnuts and broken glass scattered on the gravel. Suddenly he was holding a murderous weapon. He held it forward like a dagger. 'Say your last prayers, preacher boy, your vision is coming true tonight.'

He expected the screaming to start, the boy to flee, his bottle to find the soft of the back, then the neck, then... but all the fear seemed to drain from the boy and he stood there, a slight wraith of a cripple.

'I am not afraid of you,' he said quietly, 'and I am not worried about dying. If it was for this life alone that I am a Christian then of all men I should be the most miserable. It is you that I am worried about. You need to take away your eyes from your problems, from the fraud that was practised on you, if that is what it was. You need to focus not on preachers but on the Christ who alone can take away your bitterness and give you peace...'

'Not again!' roared Legris as he received all the provocation he needed to do the deed. He charged at the boy, putting all the years of his frustrations and failures into those three paces. He raised his killing hand, bringing it down with all the venom he had for his father-in-law's castration of him, his wife's betrayal of him, his children's rejection of him. He actually snarled as he covered the distance between him and the boy, faces flashed before him, the unctuous face of the president promising an economy he never delivered, the fishwife's kola-stained grimace, the caretaker's merciless eyes, his section boss' sadistic smile, the condescension of all those hundreds of snobs on whose mercy he had fallen through his terrible years.

Then, as he plunged the bottle down on the defenceless head, the boy's composure broke and he screamed... and Legris saw that the provocation was not enough.

There was still a germ of something inside him that would not let him cross the threshold. In an instant of grace he saw spread out before him the canvas of a life whose problems would not go away because he had killed one fraud. As the boy's spread palms quaked in fright, inches from the bottle's jagged edges, Legris saw his homelessness, his hopelessness, his grief. — At the very last moment he turned away, knocking the preacher to the ground with his bulk, turning away the hungry edges of glass.

Legris hit the gravel and rolled into a clumsy heap. He was panting. The bottle had fractured on the ground and he had glass fragments and blood in his hand. His own blood. He pulled out the slivers of glass in his palm and made a fist on his handkerchief. He put his hands between his legs. He trembled.

The preacher was weeping on his knees. 'Mister...'

'Go away, now,' said Legris. There was something about his tone that did not brook discussion. The preacher struggled to his feet and stood swaying for a moment. He was burning with the shame of an anointing that had fled at the crunch. He was without composure, completely disoriented by the turn of events, by his narrow deliverance from a death he had desired, despised, and in the nick, become terrified of. Yet, he fell back on the force of habit.

'Can we pra...'

'I think maybe you are the devil himself, provoking me to kill you.'

At that the preacher turned, he picked up his Bible, which had fallen to the ground, and stumbled away.

The rage had gone. He had shown up the preacher as a fraud peddling pipe-dreams, yet all that was left was a black despair. He had punctured an idiot's vision but it did not make his own reality any more palatable. He could not go back home. There was nobody to turn to. His nose was assailed by the overwhelming pong of smelly fish and kaushe soup, which had somehow impregnated his clothes and skin. He felt an overmastering revulsion at himself. From the depths of his being he despised himself. He hated himself.

It was over for him.

In the darkness beyond he began to hear a characteristic nattering and he knew that the preacher was praying. Yet, even that disobedience of his express wishes could not deflect his coursing self-loathing. The preacher was like a noisy fly buzzing annoyingly on a windshield; but it was Legris himself that Legris could not live with.

In the distance the atmosphere began to change. The night began to sing, the earth trembled, an eerie cry sighed through the air. A minute passed and the trembling of the world consolidated upon the rail track. Legris raised his eyes and three hundred metres away he saw the one-eyed locomotive pounding towards him.

Without a single moment of thought the plan became complete in his head. It was the sort of offer that came upon one without warning or planning. A street-hawker steps up suddenly in a traffic hold up; offers a stolen Rolex for a song. Will you buy or not? Out of the blues. A second to decide before the traffic moves along. A lifetime to regret if you decided wrongly.

He waited until the last possible minute then rose to his feet like a man who was running late for an appointment. He hurried to meet the rushing train. There was a scream of a foghorn, or something, there was a clash of brakes then there was the terrible, terrible impact, and he knew nothing anymore...

*

The preacher waited until the interstate bus had entered well on its journey before rising to his feet and limping to the head of the aisle. Just behind the driver's cabin, he turned to face his fifty or so fellow travellers. He was carrying a worn Bible with thick black rubber band around it. 'Praise Jesus,' he said.

'Oh no!' sighed a fat woman two seats down the aisle from him, 'Not again!'

'Yes, again,' said the preacher and when the woman looked up pugnaciously, she saw in the face of the man something that she had never seen before in the interminable succession of itinerant preachers that harangued her on journeys. She saw a face that had known grief, sitting within a shroud of almost unattainable peace. She listened.

They all listened.

'Please pass this around,' said the preacher, and they did; a sobering silence fell upon the bus as it sung on towards the south.

'What I am telling you, is not a figment. It is not something I read in a book, no matter how holy. It is something I personally experienced. Somebody died that I might live. Somebody bore a punishment that was meant for me.' The preacher lifted the Bible. 'And he did it to make real for me what was written in his book. You are looking at a photograph of his mutilated body; it is going to be the most famous body in this country. It will be even more famous than many presidents, so help me God.'

Sixty kilometres on, Legris debarked at Mokwa, having imparted some of his peace, his wonder and his faith in The Lamb to the travellers.

The fat woman had pressed some money into his hand, enough for more reprints, enough for the next bus fare. He made the prints before he limped into the bus park, favouring the leg he had broken six months earlier when the preacher had pushed him off the railway track. His eyes were burning with missionary zeal. He was praying silently as he waited to be led to another bus.

Ψ

There was a single whistle from the veranda and Njide goose-pimpled, just to hear it. It was Kanu's highest compliment and it took her back decades. The old woman's eyes were still shut when Njide finished her tale, her chest rising and falling rhythmically. She was either fast asleep or shamming, reluctant to postmortem any more stories. Whatever, Njide felt foolish, like someone who had finished a lengthy telephone explanation only to realise that the connection had been long broken.

Ezinne tiptoed in as Njide stretched out a hand to wake Ma'K`anu. Shhh! she whispered, waving a hand. Let her sleep.

They drew a coverlet up to her chin and gently propped her higher on the pillows. They regarded the old woman for a while then Njide glanced at the clock. It was 5 am.

I think the wake is over, she said.

On the veranda, boots and floorboards creaked as the rest of the family returned to the broken-down car at the gate. Njide frowned. They should come in.

They won't, said Ezinne simply. She lay on one side of the large poster bed and Njide took the other. Just before she dropped off, the schoolteacher propped herself up on an elbow and met her sister's eyes over the lined, peaceful face of their foster mother. That story, she smiled quietly, I know it's renewed her mind like Legris'. Just you wait till morning!

Ezinne lay back and was silent. Presently, her breathing became more rhythmic as she fell asleep. Njide was also silent for a long time, listening to the faint wheezing from Ma'Kanu, the creaks from the sleeping house, and the family of rats in the ceiling making hay with lightning raids on the kitchen. The muslin in Tobe's unfinished door rose and fell, letting through a cold breeze and the exertions of an insomniac cockerel. She began to think of all the unfinished things in her life and her eyes filled with tears. Thoughts of self-pity pursued and overtook her. She had wanted to be an actress but she had married a banker for whom the very thought was anathema.

Indeed, she'd had an auditioning for a home video scheduled when they met but she'd never kept the appointment. The honeymoon had continued until eleven months into the marriage when he lost his job. Another miserable year passed before desperation drove him into a job in a pools office. The blot of the pools office on his CV kept him out of banking thereafter and his depression found a vent in alcoholism. And in punching sessions with his actress wife, typecast in the role of punching bag.

An unfinished audition, an unfinished career, an unfinished honeymoon… she blinked back her tears angrily. She was at the wake of a dying woman unprepared for eternity, and all she could think of was herself!

She recalled an anachronistic Odozi proverb: only witches could sleep at the wake of a beloved. Solemnly she resolved that if it was the last thing she would do for Ma'Kanu she would keep the wake until the break of dawn. There was so much to pray for, so much to remember.

So resolving, she fell soundly asleep.

THE SCATTERING

ψ

Somto could not sleep. The stories of the night rolled over him like huge waves in a calming sea he'd almost forgotten how to swim, but there was one tale that whammed through his being with the concussive force of a sonic boom. *Silence in Heaven* filled him with the lead of despair, numbing his mind and putting a shameful sense into his existence. He rejected it with all that he had, and yet it was only by owning up to the scandalous truth of his ancestry that he could understand his unravelling life. He ran his jeep off the road and onto the grassy verge in front of the Community School. He switched off the engine, welcoming the silence that followed his guttural engine. He locked up the jeep and began to walk.

It was cold out on the scarp lands. The streets were quiet but far from deserted. Every other lane had its regulation couple telling earnest things to each other. He passed drunks making their circuitous way home from the distant funeral. He headed for the hundred and twenty year old Sisters of Mercy Convent. As he approached it, the dome of the main hall rose steadily until it blocked the moon from his horizon and he was standing in a blanched shadow. The trellises of several aging roses covered the north approach. A rhododendron hedge defined a grotto in the central quadrangle.

He stood in front of the gate for several minutes, knowing how unreasonable it was to knock on the gates of a convent at that time, and yet unable to help himself. As he psyched himself up to the sacrilege of knocking, an old night watchman appeared from the shadow of a pillar and the gate creaked open. Somto realised that he had been the subject of the guard's scrutiny. Yes? demanded the old man suspiciously.

I have to see the Mother Superior.

Are you mad? Do you know the time?

Normally, it required more than a rash inquiry to provoke Somto, but he seemed like an incontinent river that had burst its banks, whose waters were now permanently on the alluvial plains. He rasped, If I were mad the time won't matter and if I'm not, it means my business is urgent, isn't it?

The guard was too sleepy to make sense of the gibberish, he shook his head. This isn't an asylum, he said, pushing the gate shut, even as Somto put his foot in the gap. It was apparent that a confrontation was in the offing, but from the silent backdrop, a quiet footfall began to emerge. The old guard turned and presently a dapper, elderly woman dressed in white stepped into the halo of light.

Although Mother Clementina was a teenager when she first entered the Odozi convent, the hair that now showed under her white hood was completely gray. She didn't look like one that had just been roused from sleep. Young man, what is it that can't wait till morning?

My name is Somto, I was one of the boys at …

I remember you.

He paused. watching her face carefully. She could deny everything, but he would see it there in her face, the confirmation that she was lying. She's told me the truth at last, he said hoarsely… then his world caved in yet again as she blinked slowly and sighed deeply. There was no denying it then.

I think you should come in, she said quietly. A nonplussed guard pulled the door wider, allowing him to enter.

The Mother Superior received him in a small cubicle as forbidding as a headmistress' office. A single print of the Holy Family hung on the wall, stapled at two lower ends by small bouquets of a pink and yellow bloom. He settled respectfully into a chair that was clearly older than he was.

She had plugged a small electric kettle on to boil before she sat down and she produced a tea service with a comportment appropriate to an ecclesiastical duty. By the time she settled two tiny cups into their saucers and had them properly accoutred with teabags and grains of sugar, the water was ready to be poured.

Somto took and sipped a cup, for want of something to do with his hands. It is true then? he asked as she settled into the chair in front of him.

Depends on what she told you.

He took a deep breath; although he brought out the sentence swiftly, there was still a detectable pause before the execrable word. That I was a product of a… rape; that I was born in this convent, that my mother abandoned me at birth.

She pulled a huge Bible down from a low shelf and placed it on her lap. Although she made no move to open it, she stroked it like one would a lover. There was a rape, yes, she began, but did you notice the flash of love as well? Like the one between Amnon and Tamar? That was in second Samuel, thirteen...

I came here for facts, snapped Somto before he could stop himself, not sermons.

She chuckled in her first smile, revealing a new face entirely, one that could have been at home behind a shop counter. Then you're in the wrong place. This is a convent, young man, not a library.

She waited, and when he made to move to go, added, You're one of the lucky ones. Post-natally depressed mothers sometimes kill their children. Your mother gave you into a loving home. You should be grateful.

I should be, he said, but I'm not. He carried the cup to his tongue and allowed the liquid to scald his tongue and course a trail of fire into him. Is there a history of post-natally deceived children indulging in homicide?

I'm sorry I have no tears to shed for you, she said firmly. Your story isn't half as tragic as those of many girls in my convent.

I don't want your tears.

And you don't want my sermon either. Her smile made her next words even softer. So what exactly do you want?

Where's she?

Why do you want to know? To indulge a spot of homicide? The woman hesitated. She rose and walked to the window. Her cup of tea had not stirred from its saucer. She looked out into the lightening sky, hugging the large Bible to herself. I don't know if I should be telling you this, but your mother didn't really abandon you. — Yes she left you within days of your birth...but she came back. A couple of years afterwards... she took a deep breath, and not just once too. Indeed I recall the last time, you were seven or eight. She looked through a gloomy window and pointed a finger at a darkened courtyard. You were standing in line for catechism with your brother, the big one, Kanu. She turned around, she said quietly. She was sitting in that very chair.

She came back for me?

Yes. Many mothers change their minds you know. I didn't think it possible, considering the depth of her feelings in the beginning. But there you are, a mother is a mother.

She came back? exclaimed Somto from his feet. Why wasn't I told?

She laughed nervously, taking an unconscious step backwards as he advanced on her. I had to take a hard decision. You were happy here in Odozi.

You played God over my life?

Ma'Kanu would have killed me rather than give up any of her children. Remember the Orachonsi episode. Besides, you were in a happy Christian home, up the street from me, I could hardly have pulled you out of that and sent you to an unknown fate with an unbalanced woman… There were no legal papers, but an adoption is a pretty final act, quite different from foster parentage...

Somto grabbed her by the shoulders, and shook her like a rag doll. His yells merged with those of the shocked woman, piercing the sanctity of the convent and the silence of the emerging dawn. Doors opened and slammed in the background, seconds passed and the door of the room broke open. A shocked woman stood there, wrapped in a blanket, soon to be joined by several others. There was no need for further intervention, Somto left the Mother Superior and backed away until he felt the window panes against his back.

Mother Clementina shakily picked up her Bible and hood from the ground. She dropped into a chair. She bowed her face into her palm for such a long time that they began to fear that she was weeping. Then she abruptly picked up her cup and sipped it deliberately. The old guard appeared, but upon seeing so many nuns inappropriately dressed he backed off gingerly.

Mother Clementina rose and stared at Somto. Her lower lip was quivering. Thirty-six years ago I did you — and your mother — a favour. Today I'll do you another one: go in peace. But don't show your face in this convent again.

He stood for several moments as the full realisation hit him. He had desisted from physical violence for two decades only to end up assaulting a nun. Slowly he dropped to his knees. He did not trust himself to speak.

Several more minutes passed and Mother Clementina sighed: Go in peace. This time, her voice held no bitterness. Somto did not move. Finally, his voice came. It was almost a whisper: I won't hurt her, I swear.

Mother Clementina's lips were sealed by her vocation. Her secrets were lodged too deep for physical pain or bodily threats to dredge. But there was something she saw in the eyes that broke through her defences. Her town was called Iria. Don't know if she's still there, this was almost thirty years ago.

Outside, the lights of an approaching truck fixed Somto for the five minutes it took to labour uphill. As its sound faded away in the direction of the quarry, Somto allowed his feet to find their way back to his jeep. His mind picked up and dropped subjects like a distracted shopper in a convenience store. The horror of his assault on the reverend woman was powerfully offset by the new hope she had handed her. He seized upon it: his mother had come back for him.

*

By morning, Cecelia Wiggle was dead.

A gold-dusted dawn had broken over the scarp lands of Milken Hill to show the rest of Chief Ude's exhausted mourners the way home. Kanu and Udeme were sleeping in the car parked outside Orphan House when Ezinne's piercing scream shredded the silence of the neighbourhood. Njide's wasn't far behind. Only the two children in the car respected Ma'Kanu's ban on tears.

The news flared through Odozi. By the time a bathing Dada snatched a towel and arrived at the gate of Grace Lodge, a dozen others had beaten her to it. They stood there indecisively for a good five minutes, straining against the restraint of the Igwe's ostracism. Then Dada howled and blundered though the gate, sobbing up to the veranda of Grace Lodge. It was the signal the villagers had been waiting for. Within minutes the house was swamped with mourners. The only people left on the street were the occupants of Kanu's car, hemmed between the fragrance of Ma'Kanu's heliotrope blossoms and the sound of children bathing at the public tap.

Hours passed.

Njide stepped carefully down from the veranda with Udeme's flowerpot in her hand. She shook her head violently to free up her tousled braids as she walked a drunken path across the far lawn. As she set the pot down near the gate, Kanu and Udeme were watching a local mechanic uncouple their carburettor. It was a hot day, and they exchanged joyless embraces, the sort close relatives shared at tragic funerals. Njide smiled wanly as she nodded at the orchid. It's truly beautiful, she said to Udeme. It will be lovely on the grave.

I'm hungry, replied Udeme, walking off towards Ekwutosia's provision stores.

Njide turned to Kanu and took a deep breath. There was a swathe of gray in his hair and a scar on his temple whose story she didn't know. What a waste of years! she was thinking, as she asked, Won't you come in?

Kanu shook his head. Below the surface, Njide could feel the resentment in the giant that came from a grief that could not be vented. For the first time, Njide felt an intruder in Grace Lodge. Although she knew it was illogical, she felt an alien, coming between mother and natural son. For ten years it had been there under the surface, the drifting apart of the children of Orphan House. For the first time, she felt the schism rising to the top.

The villagers are there, urged Njide. *You* ought to be there.

Kanu shook his head again. Once the car is fixed we'll be gone for good. I've snatched enough sleep for the drive home.

And Grace Lodge? What happens to Grace Lodge? We had plans for it, don't you remember? Now it's up to Ezi and I?

There's not much grace left here, said Kanu bleakly. That's how she wanted it.

There was a long silence, then Njide crossed the road and went down the hill, away from the old convent. Where are you going? asked Kanu without a great deal of interest.

She paused but didn't turn around. The council house. We need a burial certificate. She was smarting from his coldness and from the quality of Udeme's rejection. She could feel a bitterness she didn't know she had, coming out in her voice and poise. She turned with an effort of will. She asked: Will you at least dig the grave? Or should I ask the villagers?

For answer, Kanu got into the car and shut the door.

*

He found the town on the borders of the desert, between Doma and Lafia. It was long past noon and he was thirsty enough to drink the water in his radiator when he saw the broken signboard that spelt 'Iria'. He turned off the expressway and rattled down the dust track that ran directly into the town.

He hung around the broken bridgehead for a long time, looking across the sixty metres of sluggish, swollen river at the lonely lane that led into the town of Iria. There was a one-car pontoon on the other side of the river whose pilot was cultivating a potbelly with a brew in a bottle. Somto had a deep foreboding about trusting his jeep to a pontoon with a pronounced starboard list. — Or striking out on foot for that matter. It was hard to articulate his unease, but it was matched by an equally overwhelming determination to seek out his forbears. His job on the rig was a distant memory. His years with Ma'Kanu at Orphan House was a vexation, a foundation of lies that irked, just to think of it.

As Ma'Kanu had related *Silence in Heaven*, there had been a re-verberating chord inside him, witness to the fact that she told the truth. It was easy for people... including Madam-Put-More, to scoff at his father's footloose mission. *He* would never scoff. He *under-stood* it from deep inside. Suddenly he *saw* why a twelve-month marriage had felt like a twelve-year jail sentence. He had tried his hands at several trades, passing his last correspondence exams in engineering the very week Getty died. He took frequent holidays, didn't put down roots and carried several changes of clothes in the rear of his jeep.

The rapist that fathered him was deeply relevant to who he was. Suddenly he wanted to know how the Stranger with no name ended up. With an empathy that did not exist the night before, he *knew* that the Stranger would have his own story, which would put the sexual transaction that created him in a different light. Surely the single-minded spirit in him was nothing more insane that the adventurous determination of the intrepid explorers of earlier centuries who drew the maps and extended the borders of the known world. Almost forty years had passed since the Stranger's fateful meal at Madam-Put-More's; Somto was filled with an unmaster-able curiosity as to whether he succeeded in his mission. If he had, he'd be near retirement, and an interesting character he'd make.

He backed the jeep up and retreated a kilometre towards the highway, to the lean-to where a family of lepers ran a car wash for articulated trucks. He pulled his jeep into an oversized bay and paid for a wash and overnight parking. He took a change of clothes. His black pouch was too valuable to leave in the glove compart-ment and he pushed it down an inner pocket before starting the short walk back to Iria.

The pontoon pilot was urinating into the Kigalo River when he reached the broken bridge. They had a shouted argument over the fare. The boatman insisted on charging an extra fare to cross the river to pick up Somto. The stalemate lasted a few minutes before a trader crossing from Iria solved the problem. The pilot cached his bottle and pushed the craft off the Iria Jetty. The crossing took fifteen minutes and the well-lubricated pilot insisted on collecting Somto's return fare in advance.

Finally they were off. The pilot talked non-stop: the men of Iria had quarried limestone for the cement factories, until the cement boom ended, when Iria started haemorrhaging not only her young but also the regular incomes they'd spent in her shops and businesses. There was a poignant hopelessness in the air of the town Somto entered, in the town that held the best credentials for his hometown. Was Madam-Put-More still alive after thirty years? Would she still be in business? And if she was, would she be the lone oasis of prosperity in the insular and decrepit town?

He trawled his mind for the locational triggers for Madam Put-More's canteen in Ma'Kanu's story. Despite his fierce thirst, he had wanted to have his first drink in the buka. But when he had walked the length of the Main Road without seeing an Esso Petrol Station, he stopped at a roadside kiosk and bought a litre of bottled water. When it was half-empty, he asked the vendor, who looked old enough to know, what happened to Iria's Esso station.

The man brightened up at the question. You don't look old enough to know an Esso! he scolded. That was decades ago they went out of business here! It's now a Unipetrol station...

Side-stepping a lengthy reminiscence, Somto found the two-pump Unipetrol station half a kilometre metre away. Standing on its forecourt, the only restaurant Somto could see was a canopied buka less than two minutes walk away. He approached it slowly, arriving more than five minutes later. It straddled the junction between Main Road and a lane that led down to a dilapidated primary school.

It did not boast a signboard. It looked as old and natural as the flame tree that stood before it. Two elderly men diced on a ludo board on one of the several tables under the tree. A bitch suckled six whining puppies by the gate, snarling as Somto passed the low entrance and entered the restaurant. An oppressive smell of oil beans hit him and he quickly decided he would not enjoy a meal there.

An itinerant shoeshiner was the only patron inside the restaurant. He was contentedly crushing the bony remnants of an indeterminate meal, his box of polish sitting on the table. There was no woman in the place. The hulking waiter struggling out of his chair was younger than Somto, and did not look overjoyed to see him. He wiped his hands on a dirty apron and placed a coaster on his interrupted beer. The pounded yam has finished, he warned, as Somto picked up a dog-eared menu, and there's no ukazi or gbegiri soup. There's drawsoup but there's no meat in it. Stewed beans is remaining only the burnt side and the farmers pottage is…

What *do* you have?

Jollof rice.

Bring it.

The man withdrew into a backroom. Of course at her age she won't come in everyday, Somto reflected; Most likely she was in semi-retirement, not in the upstairs loft, which would explain the run-down buka and atrocious service. Alone with the shoeshiner, Somto sat down, feeling a strange clumsiness settle on him: an absence of the usual composure he was able to wear – and fake though life. His hands were clammy and hot, he seemed unable to find the right way to cross his legs, and… damn that smell of oil beans! After a while, Somto decided that he was the subject of a more than casual scrutiny. He turned in the direction of the shoeshine man who asked, his voice an earnest squeak: 'Want a shine, mister?'

No.

As it's so late, I'll give you one for half price.

I said no! snapped Somto, then, realizing how curt his nervousness had made him sound, he shrugged and added: No money.

The shoeshine man continued to study Somto. He was small-boned and balding, dressed in weathered, blue dungarees that contrasted sharply with Somto's bright new orange overalls. He had quick, cunning eyes, and an expressive face. He also had an irritating tic: a quick sideways and upright glance that gave him the furtive air of a monkey. He had stayed several years too long in a lazy job and had got stuck in it for life. He gave his fingers a final lick as he seemed to make up his mind. He rinsed briskly in a bowl of water. Okay, just give me anything you like.

With that he rose and, over Somto's protests, prisoned the engineer's foot in a leg lock while he administered a shoeshine from an empty tin of boot-polish. Before Somto's meal was ready, his boots had lost their dust cover, even if they were still lacking a polish. His smallest note was too large for a shoeshine and he reluctantly produced it to the man for some change. The shoeshiner made it disappear and grinned lopsidedly at his client. God bless you! And you were pretending to be broke! Thanks, that was double my fees!

Where's my change? demanded Somto, a little embarrassed.

The other man's eyes widened in amazement. You want your change? He shrugged and upended a bag of the smallest denomination coins, which would be spurned by any self-respecting beggar. He began to arrange rows of tens, sniffing all the while: You're more than this, nobody *ever* asks for change.

Somto relented. Go on, get out of here, you rascal,

But the man had other plans. He swiftly stowed his bag of coins and clicked the metal handle of his shoeshine box deprecatingly: This is just my part-time job. Anything you want in Iria, I can fix it. You look like a stone prospector, I can link you up...

The tall waiter slouched in with Somto's food, his lips curled up in a corner, Don't be starting again, Moonshine.

...but maybe you're a tourist, said the shoeshiner, ignoring the interruption, if it's a hotel you're needing, I can take you to Iria's cheapest and cleanest, yes?

The meal was indifferent and Somto decided that the smell of oil beans was related to the person of the waiter, who seemed to have an unresolved issue with a hangover. He had settled in to resume his beer only to slip gently asleep. Despite his hunger, Somto managed only a couple of spoons. Finally, he dredged the casualness to ask the question that brought him three hundred circuitous kilometres: Where's Madam-Put-More?

The shoeshine man dispensed the answer without thinking, unaware of the potential effect those words could have on his prospects for further commissions for the rest of that night: Between heaven and hell, I'm sure. Eh, Stevo? he rapped the waiter's table, Didn't Madam PM's last stroke kill her?

The words careened drunkenly through Somto's mind. *There was a Madam-Put-More!* He tensed as the pendulum swung between life and death.

The waiter shrugged indifferently without opening his eyes.

Isn't she the owner of this buka? Somto asked.

That roused Stevo. The owner? he demanded, taking offence, So what does that make me? A common waiter? He put a foot on the table to make his point as he took the coaster off his beer.

Moonshine looked at Somto through narrowed eyes. You're not a stranger to Iria, he said accusing. Madam PM sold this place more than ten years ago. Stevo bought it from the man who bought it from her.

Where's she now?

She was in hospital in Lafia when she had her last stroke. That was years ago. She must be dead by now.

Somto didn't have a clear recollection of leaving the restaurant, but presently he found himself following Moonshine down an alley, away from the Main Road that ran parallel to the Kigalo. After a twenty-minute walk, he paused outside the Cornerstone Hotel, a four-room brothel that masqueraded as a bed-and-breakfast. She might be gone, but the town was still his root. He would spend the night at least, get to know the place. He looked up to see a curious set of eyes trained on him. That's why you're here, isn't it? What was your business with Madam-Put-More?

That's between Madam-Put-More and I, he replied easily.

I used to do a creditor's tour of Iria, sighed Moonshine, but you're very, very late now. You won't find anything now.

Somto found himself paying twice Moonshine's original estimate for the 'best room' in the hotel: it did have a view of the Kigalo, but between his window and the river was what looked and smelled like the hotel's rubbish dump. Later that evening, resident rats were to make sleep a trial. Just then, all Somto said was: It will do.

Moonshine hung around until he got an adequate tip.

You have a head for money, grudged Somto, You must be rich.

The other man's face clouded over. Iria's beer parlours are rich, he said, turning and carrying his little clapper-box downstairs.

Somto backed into his room. He had catnapped in truck stops along the way to Iria, but his two days of driving through punishing terrain had exhausted him. All he wanted right then was to fall asleep. But once he'd unlaced his boots and fallen into the bed, he found himself worrying, unaccountably, about Ma'Kanu — whether she was dead or alive. Angrily, he lurched out of bed and headed downstairs. He hadn't travelled all that way for an early night anyway. He saw Moonshine, back towards him, importuning the hotel's proprietor for an introductory commission, as he slipped out of the Cornerstone Hotel and followed the Kigalo.

The Kigalo River was lazy and sprawling in its swathe through Iria. Although deep in places, its currents were too slow to drown an adult without his full cooperation. Iria's Main Road had also acquired meanders by running parallel to The Kigalo, but the river seemed a more scenic route to walk. Thirty minutes from the lodge,

Somto paused under an India rubber tree to watch a small river market. Fifteen to twenty canoes were berthed on a large sandbank and some three score people huddled around mounds of grains, yams and spices. Further up the bank stood several stalls surrounded by haggling customers. Somto paused by the throng and listened to the alien drone of a strange language; gradually his mind drifted back to the story, *Silence in Heaven*.

In the years during which it was taboo to question Ma'Kanu on the issue of origins, Givemore had been his only recourse. The old man had a strange fascination with Orphan House, somehow he had acquired the most obscure information about her residents. He was a decade or two older than Ma'Kanu and although he did know something about her past, he was so completely overawed by her that he never divulged a whit. The name Margarita had come from Ma'Kanu's Bible, and the fire that killed her brothers had slipped out of her in the course of a fever-induced delirium shortly after Kanu's thirteenth birthday.

However, Somto had learnt all Givemore knew about him; which wasn't all that much. Somto had been born in the convent, of a tall, beautiful woman whom Givemore had never seen before and had never seen since. That mysterious woman had been the substrate of a few million dreams. Thinking back, he realised that Givemore's account corroborated *Silence in Heaven*. The truth had come with a twist he could never have imagined in his worst nightmare.

Whatever else he might discover, this was his root. He had found the place of his conception; and although it was an act of hate, not of love, it was up there in the loft above the sleepy restaurant. The river market was drawing to a precipitous close and while the traders on the sandbank packed their wares into the canoes and pulled away, more stalls were appearing on the street, each one furnished by an oil lamp. Somto pushed himself away from the tree trunk. A dark night was falling, a night made doubly mysterious by the unfamiliarity of his surroundings. He began to walk.

As he walked, he found himself looking more searchingly at people than he had ever done before. A man with a gray-streaked beard peeled away from a wall and importuned Somto for some coins. He looked fierce but his voice was quiet and timid; what was the story of his life? A snoring drunk in three layers of clothing rolled over beside a suya brazier, bringing meat, powdery coal and curses showering down on him. What track had he walked? From her stall, a middle-aged trader cracked a bawdry joke... another chewed gum viciously... The layerings and dimensions of life suddenly overwhelmed him. He felt deeply knit with the people, any of whom could have been a distant relation, and yet alone. Like a man with a hallucinogen in his bloodstream, he was reading meanings into the meaningless. He crossed the Main Road and walked deeper into Iria, through narrow streets that seemed to stray through private compounds and public bathrooms, drawn by a tumult that rose from deep inside the native quarters.

It was a wedding celebration. It sprawled out from an epicentre in a kind of village square choked on every side by small, balconied bungalows. On every spoke of the six or seven streets that spun away from the square, villagers sat or loitered. Somto followed the street that brought him there, all the way to the square, to the musicians, whose music had drawn him. Around them, dancers hustled, vibrating their shoulders in that lazy manner that he soon found was idiosyncratic of Iria.

The bride soon stumbled upon him. She was a long-boned woman with a distracted air who stood out from her fellows by her height and extravagant attire. She was doing the last dance; escorted by a bevy of maidens, she did a dance circuit around the square, to the accompaniment of wolf calls and whistles. She came close to Somto and paused. The maidens surrounded the bemused man. Then she came closer, still dancing, and said over the din of the drums: Hi Stranger.

He nodded. And suddenly the synapses clicked. His father had been known as 'The Stranger'.

There was a wayward headiness in the drumbeat that Somto could feel himself, and he knew that the woman's words were half the exhilaration of the music and half the ritual of a final flirtation: If you arrived yesterday, she said, her mouth in a self-willed pout, I won't be getting married today.

Then she danced away. He watched her go, conscious that not a few bystanders had overheard her words. He was still staring after her when Moonshine sidled up to him. Don't take her serious, he counselled. He had replaced his tattered dungarees with a tattered danshiki and unfashionable bell-bottoms. She's supposed to say that to everybody.

From the hostile glares of the wedding guests around him, Somto doubted that it was a well-known custom. Take me to the drummers, he said, switching the topic.

Why?

Somto shrugged; and shrugged again. Then he surrendered to the intoxication of the music, continuing the rhythmic shoulder-dance of the Iria. Moonshine looked at him curiously, but he led the way past the staring villagers to the percussionists' stand.

They weren't like any drums he had ever played before. Three percussionists manned the stall, each playing an array of local drums that ranged in size from cup to bucket. Yet, despite the puny dimensions of their equipment, the orchestral impact of three drum sets playing a complementary but unidentical tatoo was immediately riveting. The spirit of the music possessed Somto. Following Moonshine, he drew closer to the clump around the drum sets.

There was a queue of three or four boys behind each array of drums. With Moonshine's intervention, he joined one. The drums were played so energetically that a drummer lasted twenty or so minutes before his fervour flagged and he was crowded out by the next on the queue. When it came to Somto's turn, he slipped onto the stool.

He played for an hour.

He shut his eyes and found the boundaries of the style, those fixed posts within which he had to play in order to remain within the culturally defined rhythm. Then he opened his eyes and, ever so gently, he pushed them back. The drumsticks triggered new reserves of energy and he found himself coursing with vitality. Unleashed from Njide's restraint, incited by the competition of the other power drummers, he translated his anger and confusion, his lonliness, his fury and his loss into a cascading tattoo on the assortment of drums.

...and he could have played forever, but he saw a flash of colour to his right and from the corner of his eyes, saw the bride approach, dance before him, and paste a succession of currency notes on his wet forehead. Many drummers had performed before him but he alone attracted that unwelcome attention, flustered, he lost his rhythm and faltered. Within seconds, he was stumbling off the stool as another drummer took his place. When he looked up she was walking away, but there was a tension in the air. He pushed into the crowd, trying to lose himself, feeling foolish and unbalanced. He could feel the subtle shift in the mood of the gathering as eyes followed him for reasons unrelated to his prowess on the drums. He looked around for Moonshine, turning first to the right and then left into a punch that snapped his head back so sharply that he staggered several paces backwards until he fetched up against a table, scattering plates and spilling drinks.

The bridegroom he had earlier seen from a distance fell on him, snapping off the legs of the table and smashing him into the ground. He was probably twice as old as his bride, and certainly twice as heavy. Somto was overwhelmed by a flurry of blows and his eyes were almost closed before the kicking man was lifted off him. Several hands helped him to his feet. Gradually, he realized that the drums had fallen silent, and with them, the rest of the musicians. The bridegroom continued to kick at him from a distance, mouthing abuse, and a huge hubbub rose on all sides. He was disoriented; and yet it was nothing serious: only his second brawl in two decades; he wasn't the aggressor, had sustained no broken bones, and had only caused the disruption of a wedding feast. — Nothing serious at all. The supporting hands left him; he turned around in a bewildered circle, seeking the familiar face of Moonshine, who was suddenly nowhere to be found.

He felt a chill as a breeze reached his skin through a tear in his overalls, a chill that deepened as he patted his rear pocket and discovered that his wallet was gone. At least he still had the pouch in his inner pocket. He pushed his way through the crush until he got beyond the square then walked down the street, trying to put distance between him and the scene of his embarrassment. He found the Kigalo, he loitered aimlessly for an hour, alternating between the impotent fury of a mugging victim and intense discomfiture, as he scrambled to find the wholeness he had felt earlier in the day when he walked that stretch of river.

The sensation was quite gone.

He picked his way carefully towards the hotel, let himself into his room and lay on the bed. Ninety minutes had passed since the bridegroom's punch almost snapped off his head, but his heart was still pounding furiously. His thoughts were now far from Ma'Kanu, but he was further from sleep than ever before. His deposit would last him until weekend, but he'd starve all the way. And for what?

The sound of knocking roused him from a sleep that had ambushed him. His watch showed that two hours had passed since he got into bed. Groggily he swung his feet off the bed, forcing a rat that was halfway across the room to change directions. He opened the door to an anxious caretaker, who stepped out of the way for a scowling man with a potbelly. The new man pushed his way into the room and looked around with a proprietary air.

What is this all about? demanded Somto,

You'll soon know, was the rude reply. Get your boots on, we're going to the station.

Is this a joke?

You'll soon know that I don't joke with my job, said the other man who was suddenly framed by two hulking policemen. Somto thought better of any resistance as he quickly pulled on his boots. He would wake up from the nightmare sooner than later, but it was still within his means to determine whether or not he did so with his dentition intact.

They rode to the police station in Inspector Vera's ramshackle Corolla. Within minutes he was sitting at a desk before the holding cells of the station, trying to justify a public affray and the gate-crashing and breaking up of a private wedding. An older man sat in one of the cells, pretending not to be listening intently to the goings-on. Somto seemed mesmerised by the second, empty cell. He was certain that his first night in his hometown wasn't also going to be his first night behind bars.

Inspector Vera turned out a decent enough fellow once he was back in his station, although he proved insufferable in his punctiliousness. As he booked Somto, he discovered he was an engineer and shifted his heavy-handedness down a gear. I thought I was dealing with a ruffian, he explained, — but what possessed you to return for a girlfriend on her wedding day? Have you no respect at all?

Is that what that mad man told you? Somto shouted, beside him with frustration, Look, all I did was play the drums and she pasted money on my head. I've never spoken a word to her in my life.

The policeman was eating fried rice out of a plastic plate with the picture of the bride and groom screen-printed on it. Uncannily, Somto's mouth filled with saliva. The inspector sniffed and looked up from Somto's statement. There's nothing here. He said. He tore several statement forms out of a pad and slid them across to Somto with a ballpoint. The top forms were soiled by his oily fingers. I want your life story, he said, ending with Izoun's present whereabouts.

Who on earth is Izoun? demanded Somto.

Inspector Vera took a swig of the bottle on his desk and replied patiently, Izoun is the man whose wife you snatched. You both disappeared after the fight, around nine-thirty. You know a wedding is no fun without the groom. The manager of your brothel says you came in at 11 pm. Can you account for your movements until then?

I was just walking around. I was upset.

Any witnesses?

Somto shrugged helplessly. Read that, said Vera, pushing across another statement with a small finger — the only one that wasn't soiled with stew.

Somto squinted at the signature on the statement. Who is Elsie?

Inspector Vera smiled humourlessly. Your girlfriend.

Somto swallowed as cold braces began to fasten themselves around his chest. He began to read. Minutes later, he had to restrain himself from ripping the statement to bits. His breath came in shallow gasps and he spoke in a voice that sounded hoarse to his own ears. Does this woman have a history of madness?

The Inspector continued to grin contemptuously.

Maybe you think *I* have a history of madness. You come into town on the very day she gets married and break up the ceremony. Tell me, he said angrily, if you didn't come for her what are you doing here? Iria isn't exactly a tourist resort.

I... can't tell you that.

You don't need to, he said, waving her statement, Because she's already told me everything. If she's never seen you before, how come she knows your name?

I don't know. Somto replied honestly enough.

Don't worry, he told Somto patronizingly, I'll get to the root of it. He rose to go, Somto rose with him. He wagged his head. You're not going anywhere. I will have to interview witnesses and they are all drunk right now. Somto's mouth dropped open.

You're not arresting me are you?

Inspector Vera sucked his teeth, showing gaps in his dentition that, at his age, suggested a more pugilistic youth. I arrested you an hour ago, but I'm offering you bail now. Do you have anyone who can stand surety for you? He grinned slyly. Your girlfriend, perhaps.

I don't know anybody in this town. Then he paused, Or, can you get me Moonshine.

The policeman looked shocked for a moment, then he shook his head as he locked Somto into the cell. He left without a word. There was a chuckle from the adjoining cell and when Somto looked across, the bearded detainee was grinning from ear to ear. That's a good one. He said eventually. I never thought I would see the day when someone cites Moonshine as a surety and character reference. You certainly know how to wreck your case.

He's the only person I know in this town! glowered Somto.

The man chuckled for a minute. Then he rolled over and extended his hand through the bars. Let's do something about that: my name is Alfonso. Alfonso Etuna.

Somto took the hand. He was still trying to figure out where he recalled the name from, when the other man locked his wrist against the bars and dispossessed him of his wristwatch. It was a swift operation and left Somto more shocked than angered. It's a cheap imitation. I would have given it to you, if you asked.

Where's the fun in that? asked the other man, I did it only for the practice. Never seen anyone who wears a watch on the right hand. He slipped the watch into a pocket without a glance. Better don't mention this to the Sarge, you seem like a man in need of friendships.

Moonshine was irredeemably drunk when he arrived at the police station and the desk sergeant refused to let him in. Alfonso woke up when the argument reached a head. He grinned at Somto who was standing at the cell door. Go to bed, my friend, he said, you're not going anywhere tonight. Somto returned to the thin foam in the corner. An hour later, Alfonso's voice came from the huddle in the corner of the other cell. You still can't sleep?

I'm thinking of my bed back in the hotel.

I have an idea that can pass the time. He said producing a pack of dog-eared cards.

My wallet was stolen in the Square, Somto told him without stirring. I have nothing you can win.

The pack of cards disappeared. You have a wrong impression of me. I'm not a criminal or anything like that, I'm just an unlucky chef. What I did to you is what the crook I met here did to me. It passes the time and who cares? Eh?

Somto sat up slowly. It clicked. An unlucky chef! Could this be the same Etuna who was Madam-Put-More's serving boy? He seemed in his fifties, which would make him just about the right age. I don't. He said thoughtfully. You've heard my story, how did *you* end up here?

It's a long story.

I've got all night. Somto told him.

THE DEVIL I KNOW

Ψ

All sorts of people go around saying things they don't understand.
I'm not like that. Me, I only say what I've seen with my own eyes; so
when I say something, you'd better listen. Folks talk such trash about
the Devil: how he's just a kind of electricity. I say, leave drivel for fairy
tales. Me, I want to talk about what is real and what I've seen with these
two eyes. Because I've met the Devil himself, and his name is Marconi
Marsi.

There's something you should understand right away, I'm not telling you what happened to me yesterday or last month. I'm going forty
years back to my student days in Boys High School, Idoti. It's less painful to reminisce now, through this long corridor of years. Idoti was a
beautiful town. (I'll talk in the past tense, because I don't know what
they've done with it now.) It had those rolling knolls and dwarf trees
that tempted us to loiter between the dormitory and the classroom —
until we fell into Mrs. Dolittle's soup...

There's a little story behind our Geography Mistress. I'll quickly tell it
here: Mrs. Dolittle was a petite Englishwoman. You'd have thought that
as a female foreigner in a tough school like Idoti High she'd have been
a walkover for us gang-lads. You'd have been dead wrong. She was the
most feared teacher, and I don't know why. Unlike the others, she didn't
believe in the cane. VP could strip your shorts and flog the skin off your
buttocks, but the kind of respect we gave Odus was nothing compared to
the fear Mrs. Dolittle inspired. Why it was like that? God knows. Of course
she had her little crazes: she came to school in rubber slippers and never
ironed her clothes. She wore no earrings in her ears, two on her brows,
and three on her nostrils alone. And she owned a dog, Goody, which she
treated like a human being. Still, she wasn't madder than Rasta-Gogi the
village loony, and we didn't fear Gogi at all.

I guess it had more to do with the power of her language — and her
gift of coming up with the most terrible aliases.

By our final year in Idoti High our buttocks were rhinoceros-hide anyway. What was Odus going to do with a koboko that would impress us?
Once, Kekere took his twelve strokes and began to snore on the assembly

bench, faking a sound sleep. Yet, the great Gonza once wet himself in class. And what made him disgrace our gang like that? Mrs. Dolittle told him to stand up.

Without condescending to vulgarisms like 'idiot', Mrs. Dolittle could rebuke the unruly for half-an-hour without repetition. The power of her language? Hah. To listen to her admonitions was like hearing your name in a vitriolic sonnet written by Shakespeare. And if she were really angry, she'd orate in French and German as well. So tell me how an Idoti teenager was supposed to endure that.

The only revenge we were capable of was secret ridicule. With all her eccentricities, she was an easy target. I don't know what was so funny about a dedicated, slightly demented teacher, but like I said, this was forty years ago. On the day Mrs. Dolittle changed his name, Jackass had gone too far with his tomfoolery. He used to be Tobi until that stupid day when he stuck paper clips on his nostrils and giggled at her back. She turned and caught him red-nosed. He had whipped the mock-earrings off so fast that he had nicked himself on the nostrils, but it was too late. She had spotted him. As she approached his desk, the only sound in the classroom was the snitching of her rubber slippers and the schadenfreude of the sniggering branches of the woolly tree fern as the wind rustled vindictively through its dry leaves. No one breathed as she circled the shaking Tobi, but she had decided on a naming, not a scolding: 'Laughing Jackass,' she said and returned to the blackboard.

The next time anyone used Tobi's real name was a week to our final exams when VP announced his expulsion for growing Marijuana on the school farm.

We used to live in dread of Mrs. Dolittle's naming ceremonies. Her aliases were sometimes comic, sometimes prophetic, but always apt. Four analgesic decades have erased the real names of some of my fellow gang-lads, but Mrs. Dolittle's aliases will stick in my memory forever, among them, Dimi (Diminutive Twerp), and Caco (Cacophonous Entity).

I should leave Mrs. Dolittle awhile. You need to meet the Devil properly. Marconi Marsi was our Literature teacher. Although the literature I learnt in one year of his teaching could have been taught in a two-hour tutorial, he had a knack for the irresistible yarn and his class was the last one anyone would stab (that was our slang for 'skip', you see). He was a handsome, self-assured man, despite his leanness; the type of person we wanted to be when we left Idoti High. He seemed too rich to be a teacher and it was rumoured that he was lying low in sleepy Idoti, being wanted over some financial skullduggery in Lagos. When he joined our school during the Harmattan term we had watched him suspiciously.

He said he didn't believe in flogging, but we weren't impressed. That was how the Chemistry Master started but soon he was competing with Odus for our koboko award.

What persuaded us was his appearance at the JSQ.

Let me first tell you about the Junior Staff Quarters. The steward's wife ran a secret beer parlour in their quarters where we rendezvoused after lights-out. She placed strict beer limits on us, knowing that just one drunken student was enough to expose her little enterprise. One night however, Marconi Marsi suddenly appeared at the entrance at midnight. We knew there were eleven dead boys in the room, because the penalty for booze in Idoti High wasn't an ordinary flogging. It was expulsion.

Marconi didn't start writing names or grabbing shirts. He simply brought out his wallet and ordered a lager from the steward's frightened wife. We quietly melted away to the dormitory to pack our bags. The following morning, VP didn't call us out at the assembly. Three gloomy days passed and the suspense was beginning to sicken us when Marconi held Kekere back after Literature class to find out why we no longer came to the JSQ. 'Drinking alone is no fun,' he said.

That was when we realised he was okay.

Devil like him.

He started bringing cigarettes to the JSQ. By May, the Marijuana cutting he gave Jackass to plant in a corner of the school farm had yielded its first harvest. You'd have thought, with all this, that his classes would have been a riot. You'd have been wrong again. I first came across the word 'diabolical' after I left Idoti High, but I recognized Marconi Marsi's middle name right away. He only had to glare at a noisemaker to plant a nightmare in his sleep. When a 'ghost' broke anything, he didn't, like VP, go whipping everyone till someone broke and betrayed the culprit. He had an instinctual sense for people's weaknesses and an ability to manipulate them. The classes of the two teachers who didn't believe in the koboko were the most organized in the whole of Idoti High, and it was a mystery to the rest of the teaching staff.

Marconi Marsi began to show his colours weeks into his arrival at JSQ. Jackass had brought a joint as usual and it was going round slowly. A week had passed since we started smoking pot and Caco was the only person in the gang who had not indulged. We were teasing him as usual but he stuck to his glass of Sprite. That was when Marconi leaned forward. I can still see the three rings of smoke he puffed, which encircled Caco before dissipating. He said, 'There's nothing you won't do, if the price is right.'

Caco shook his head. 'I'll never smoke weed.' He said simply, and I believed him. We'd been boozing for a year and he had managed to desist. I guess everyone has to learn to cage his family demons. Caco's drunken father had died in a head-on collision and the man we knew as Rasta Gogi was actually his elder brother, who had dropped out of University with a drug problem. I suppose in his shoes I'd have sworn all manner of oaths to my mum as well.

Marconi simply put twenty naira on the table. 'That's your price,' he said. 'One puff, and it's yours.' Then he turned back to a Lagos yarn he was spinning to Dimi.

Let me now tell you about twenty naira back in the '70s. I know twenty naira won't buy a pack of cigarettes today, but back then, there was nothing in our provision store that five naira couldn't buy. Let me put it this way: ten naira could increase an average student's height by six to seven inches. Twenty naira? For that money I could get VP to dance for me. Yet, there it was on the table, hypnotizing Caco. I realised there was something in the rumours about Marconi. Well, Caco didn't touch the weed. He practically rose and fled. Marconi pocketed his money. He was smiling but I think he realised that he'd lost face.

The next day, the twenty naira came out again as Jackass lit the joint. As usual Caco continued to pass it without puffing. 'What you're breathing from the air is more than the smoke in one small puff!' tempted the Devil, 'Don't be a fool, this is easy money!'

The next time the joint passed Caco, he took it to his lips. He took a deep inhalation and passed it on, letting the smoke drift out slowly though his mouth. He took the money with shaking hands and after that, the joint never skipped him again. Of course, he was never to graduate with us. Within months of that first puff of pot he had rape and theft charges hanging onto him and had become a greater menace than his brother Rasta Gogi; but that's clearly another story.

Why do gangs gather, if not to dare themselves? You'd have thought that the presence of a teacher in our midst would have dampened our dares — but by now you'd have known better. It wasn't quite three days after Caco's first puff that Odus bought his car. He was actually the Principal of Idoti High, but he'd been VP for ages and we just continued to call him that. When his car loan came through, all it could have bought, brand-new, was a motorcycle, so he opted for a fifteen-year old Datsun, which had done time as a taxi in Abeokuta. He painted the car before taking delivery and was so enamoured of it that, crazy as it sounded, he washed the car personally, every blessed morning. Yes, I'm talking about the principal of a school with three thousand students actually washing his car himself.

Odus' car arrived in Idoti High to great fanfare, at a time when there was no running water in the school. We considered how many water pipes the car loan could have laid and resolved immediately that the vehicle should not prosper. We debated puncturing a tyre, or breaking off the stalk of the aerial, but none of our ideas prospered in the face of the reality that any prank on Odus' car would lead to certain expulsion.

'The best thing,' said Marconi Marsi 'is to pour a bottle of brake fluid into his bucket before he washes his car.'

There was silence in the JSQ. Every night, the works prefects deposited two buckets of water by the car, to enable Odus to massage his ego at the crack of dawn. It was truly the perfect prank, a damage inflicted by VP with his own hands. Yet, the magnitude of the injury was far beyond our teenage animosities and gangster-aspirations. We continued to exchange glances, knowing very well that there was no love lost between Marconi and Odus. Marconi would simply be using us to settle scores. 'That's the best thing,' he repeated, this time, staring at Kekere.

Kekere had the best current reason to loathe Odus. He was the most fearless of us, and the leader of the First Eleven gang, but in pretending to fall asleep under VP's koboko he had created a cunning enemy. The Principal had delayed Kekere's next punishment until the visit of the debating team from Regan Girls Comprehensive. He had administered his strip-down flogging before those fair eyes. Weeks afterwards, Kekere was still smarting from the humiliation. Yet, it didn't make him crazy. 'That's expulsion,' he muttered.

'He'll never know who did it; and he can't expel the whole school,' said Marconi reasonably enough. He pulled out his wallet and put fifty naira on the table. We stopped breathing. At that moment I had no iota of doubt about the rumours. 'That's the price of the deed,' said Marconi.

No one touched the money.

A gang is no more a gang when everyone stands accused of cowardice. We rose for the dorm, but as we left, Marconi said he was leaving the money and the brake fluid inside the rain gauge in the Weather Garden, and anyone who wanted could take it. 'No one will ever know who.'

I didn't return to JSQ the next day. Or the day after. For a week I kept away. I thought I was fighting the demon of Mammon; if only I knew it was the Devil himself! Fifty naira! The thought of the money in the rain gauge gave me a new contempt for property. I entered the provision store and I asked the prices of things far beyond my means, considered them, and then appeared to change my mind. I took on the mentality of someone about to come into an inheritance. It was a matter of when, not if…

Yet, for all our airs, we weren't gangsters. We were merely ex-team-mates on the Idoti first eleven. In our fourth year, we had played Command School Karfi, whipping them silly. Socialising after the match, we learnt that our opponents got fifty kobo match allowances from their principal. It seemed such a perversion of the spirit of fairness: a princely fifty kobo for the losers and nothing for the triumphant winners. It soured our victory for us. We returned to Idoti and Kekere developed the temerity to ask Odus for a match allowance. That earned us twelve furious strokes apiece, a dismissal from the Idoti football team — with other punishments to follow if we were ever spotted kicking leather on the premises of Idoti High. So we went underground, that's what we did.

Looking back now from the real world, I see that, though all the germs were present, the world is manifestly more malevolent than our most depraved imagination. For all the resentment his regular caning provoked in us, we were far too innocent to contemplate the agony Marconi's plot would have provoked in Odus. The temptation operating in my mind was to take the fifty naira and pour the brake fluid down the latrine. Three things held me back: honour among thieves, Marconi's piercing eyes, and the difficulty of spending a secret naira in Idoti High.

Suddenly, it was too late. One 4 am, a week after Marconi's dare, Sheka punched my shoulder, with his hand over my mouth. I opened my eyes as he hissed in my ears: 'He's gone to the Weather Garden!'

'Who? Who!'

'Kekere!'

Then he was gone. I lay tensely in the darkness of the dormitory. Fifteen minutes afterwards, a figure stole in and padded over to Kekere's bed. I was racked by self-hate and fury, for in my mind, the money had been mine already. What could Marconi have done to me? He didn't flog, had no power of expulsion, and could hardly have reported to Odus. Then the bell prefect rang the first bell and we got out of bed.

We were still in the bathrooms when Odus started howling from the Senior Staff Quarters. Idoti High had to live with his blood-curdling bellows for the next few weeks. The prank was a complete success, as pranks went. Odus' car looked like the canvas of a demented painter.

I stared at Marconi's peaceful face throughout VP's tirade; that was how I realized it wasn't Mammon we'd been battling all along, it was the Devil himself. VP marched up and down the assembly, threatening every punishment under the sun. He gave the culprit a chance to confess. If he did so he'd get a hundred strokes spread over a week, and a month's suspension to enable his parents to fix the car. If there were no confession, when he caught the criminal it would be a line-up flogging from all the teachers in the school, expulsion and police prosecution.

Then he counted to ten; and of course there was no confession. He began to rave, snapping an apoplectic koboko in the air. Finally he dismissed the assembly and slapped the most onerous punishment ever on the entire school, till someone should betray the culprit. It was a terrible punishment. Every morning we took to the fields with machetes and worked for an hour. In the evening, we did the same for two hours. He yanked our favourite fried plantain off the menu and those that did not weep in the fields broke down in the refectory. We began to contemplate writing anonymous letters to the Ministry of Education to report our Principal for insanity. The only happy face in the school was Marconi Marsi's.

Kekere started spending his money immediately. It wasn't the spending of the money that offended me. It was the fact that whenever he got to the provision store, he bought a drink for everyone he met there. Think on this carefully, to see if Kekere didn't bring his ruin on his own head. Now he was currying popularity with the entire school, whereas, we his gang members, who knew why we were all suffering, got nothing.

I went to the JSQ that night. Jackass had two joints circulating at the same time. We were all under fifteen, yet it was there in the illegal beer parlour of the steward's wife that I first witnessed the leavening effect of wealth on a human, as he overnight outgrew his bosom companionships. A fight was on when Marconi arrived. Caco had asked a one naira fifty kobo loan of Kekere, to help him through a bad patch. Kekere had laughed, the rich man with no ambition to eliminate poverty from the world. 'If I start dividing it like that, what will be left by tomorrow?'

'Look at my hands!' raged Caco, showing the blisters from his workout on the fields. 'All this is because of you!'

Kekere spread his own palms. 'So? The money was waiting for one week, and you were too much of a coward to take it.'

That was when Marconi entered. He took Kekere's side, saying that in the world outside Idoti High, we couldn't become rich by waiting for others to take risks and share their profits with us.

Caco was flushed by a glass of beer and fifteen minutes of pot. 'We're a gang,' he snarled, 'we do things together.'

'And I'm your patron saint,' said Marconi. Devil like him! He brought out his wallet, 'I'll give you an opportunity to get rich together.' I began to sweat as he counted seventy-five naira onto the top of the table.

'What do I have to do?' Caco panted.

Marconi crumpled the foil and passed a new pack of cigarettes around. It was almost empty when it came back to him. He put a stick in his mouth and as he waited for his silver lighter to come back, he asked playfully, his eyes half closing from the smoke in the room. 'Who's the proudest person in this school?'

There were one or two suggestions then someone asked, 'Mrs. Dolittle?'

He nodded. 'Any ideas? For a prank that can knock her off her high horse?'

Ntui, who used to keep the goal, suggested that someone could hook a nail to the toilet door when she was inside to make her cry for help. But it was half-heartedly offered, for the truth was that nobody, really, wanted to humiliate Mrs. Dolittle. Apart from the fact that it was a course of action fraught with risks, (six of us in that room, including Marconi himself and I, were bearing derogatory aliases dispensed by her) the truth was that we respected her enormously. She knew her subject, which was more than could be said for Marconi, and communicated it with a passion that took every interruption of her class personally. As we drew closer to a final examination, administered by an external council rather than a crony, we began to appreciate a teacher who really could teach. In a sense, pranking Mrs. Dolittle was like tripping up a blind man. We may have been gangsters, but we drew the line somewhere.

Yet, there was the matter of the money on the table.

'That's childish,' said Marconi. He paused and lit his cigarette, working only one side of his face, intriguingly, like a bellows, 'You know that polythene bag she always carries in her purse?'

'To pick up Goody's shit?' asked Ntui, trying to work his cigarette like Marconi.

'Exactly. You know how she manages to do it with stupid dignity, as if it's not shit after all. Now imagine if Goody has diarrhoea...' he looked around the table, growing his smile, trying to be infectious, 'imagine her going around the school, scraping up after the big-for-nothing beast,' he began to chuckle uncontrollably. 'She'll have her own nickname that day: Daysoilwoman!'

I realised then that the giving of aliases was an art form not given to all. For a start, it was thoroughly beyond Marconi. He noticed that no one else was smiling. 'Come on boys,' he snorted, 'you're not pitying the dog are you? That bitch eats more meat in a week than any of you have eaten in your life.'

I could see the eyes of the frustrated First Eleven on the money as the joints passed around the table, growing shorter with every circuit. 'That's true,' owned Sheka.

'How will the dog get diarrhoea?' asked Gonza, and I realised that we had moved from the 'why' of it to the 'how'.

'Simple, I'll fry a piece of meat in castor oil and the next rich boy in this room will feed it to the dog.'

I could hear the blades of jealousy grinding in his voice; I could see the smoke from the burning hatred in his eyes, like frying oil greedily waiting for the swish of unsuspecting food. In that little vision of his eyes, I saw far more wickedness than could be externalised by a koboko. He was not a teacher, any more than a man could become a farmer by picking up a hoe. I saw why he didn't flog. For VP's flogging and Mrs. Dolittle's tongue-lashing herded us onto a path from which he would have us stray. I stubbed out his cigarette slowly. 'None of us will do it.' I told him, realizing once again that I didn't need to fear him, if he went to Odus, he'd have a lot more to answer for. — And our next Literature examinations were scheduled to be marked by an external examiner.

Marconi laughed. He drained his glass and rose. It was his shortest visit to the JSQ ever. 'For the price of seventy-five naira,' he said confidently, 'one of you will. Give me two hours to fry the meat and put everything in the usual place.' The joint reached him as he spoke and he paused to take a final pull. He opened his eyes lazily. He wasn't really that handsome. It was more confidence; that was what it was, raw confidence. The kind that Gonza needed; Gonza, the most handsome boy in the school, who changed the way he walked after every new movie he watched. Marconi lived as if he were acting a movie. Every action he took was gracious and ostentatious, inviting emulation. He began to pass on the joint to Caco, changed his mind, and converted the gesture to a pat on the back. 'Don't be slow this time,' he warned and walked away.

As I watched him go that night I saw beyond the grace and ostentation of his gestures, to the stick limbs and brittle banality that had inspired Mrs. Dolittle, at that staff get-together to welcome the new Literature teacher. He had become over-familiar with the bottle of gin, before tipsily asking her to dance, a presumptuous palm on her backside. She had icily explained that she did not dance with Macaroni, preferring to eat it for dinner. The next day, at the assembly, VP was introducing him to the students of Idoti High when he faltered at the first name — and stammered 'Mar-co-ni'. We never discovered his real name, and he never forgot why.

We didn't either. We talked late into the night, discussing Marconi's motivation and the source of his questionable wealth. Despite the formidable bribe, the thought of sickening Goody rubbed us wrong. The knifing of a dumb creature went against the grain of our unarticulated code. Although we ridiculed Mrs. Dolittle's childish infatuation with a beast that sat outside her classes and dogged her steps to and from the toilet, truth was, the excessive attention that was its lot had given it an equable temper rare in a beast of its dimensions. You could sneak up to Goody when Mrs. Dolittle's back was turned and sport with its lush hair with no danger from his formidable fangs.

We talked that matter in every direction and it was clear that soon it would be midnight and we would go away, until the small hours when the lust for money would bring someone out of bed to do Marconi's dirty work. It was a little before midnight when Kekere did what made him the leader of our gang. He stood up and pulled the remainder of his fortune from his pocket. He slapped it down in front of me. 'Judas, divide it equally.' he said, with the bravura of the hero of the Western we watched in the school hall the evening before. 'One for all and all for one.'

'All for one and one for all,' we chorused. We had hit our ceiling with the steward's wife but Ntui went to wheedle an extra bottle.

'And nobody goes near that rain gauge.' said Kekere.

The next day, we served our punishment cheerfully with the rest of the school and watched the Weather Garden like hawks. None of us went near it. VP raged at assembly, promising any informer who ratted on the vandal a month of day passes. Three days later, he added a five-naira reward. If only he knew. To avoid Marconi Marsi, we stayed away from the JSQ and began to stab his classes as well. (In any case it was only six weeks before our final exams, and frankly, his classes were a distraction to effective study.) Every time I passed Goody I felt a flush of piety at the thought of the seventy-five naira we had passed up for his health.

The feeling didn't last.

One week passed before Marconi played his trump. When I entered the class in the morning a cryptic equation that would have made sense only to eleven students in the school was scribbled on the blackboard: Fresh meat + 100 naira = Usual place. I looked around, there was no member of the First Eleven around and I wiped the board clean. Yet, over the next two days, I kept seeing the messages... and I knew that the others must have seen them too. I began to pray for our final exams.

We were going to pieces.

Listen to me: In the beginning, all I committed to was to play right-full-back in the first eleven. We'd started out the most envied and talented boys in Idoti High. Even when we were banned, we managed to make our outlawry desirable, splitting beers, stabbing classes, making rules to make us more special than the others... innocent fun, but no longer. Here I was in hell itself. Now I sat in class, trying to focus on my final revisions, and fighting a craving to raid Jackass' locker for a joint.

Caco was first to crack. He was getting into fights with everybody. Three weeks to the final exams, he broke a prefect's arm and went on suspension. He was to take the exams from outside — on condition that the prefect was also well enough to write them — but he didn't give himself that chance. The very next day he tried to rape a girl on his street. He was in jail when we took the exams.

Kekere was next. It happened out of the blues. Instead of his usual tirade, VP appeared on the assembly that morning mean and silent. He called out Kekere and presented him to us as a future highway robber and murderer who was certainly not going to graduate from Idoti High. When Kekere saw the eleven teachers lined up with kobokos, waiting for the end of the Principal's tirade, he lost his nerve and did a three hundred metre dash across the field, outrunning the best runners in the school and taking the wall in a single, flawless vault. The mass punishment for the whole school ended that day and we never saw Kekere again.

I still don't know which of us took the reward for his betrayal.

I suppose it was the furore over Kekere's fate that broke our surveillance of the Weather Garden. By the time a first-year boy ran into Mrs. Dolittle's class to raise the alarm, it was too late. Goody was retching and whining and the whole school was gathering. I saw then, what I should have known, knowing Marconi Marsi for whom he was: that Marconi's antipathy towards Mrs. Dolittle wasn't something that could be doused by a dog's diarrhoea.

By nightfall, Idoti High was venue of the best-attended dog's burial I ever saw. The less said about Mrs. Dolittle, the better. Even forty years isn't enough to dull the pain. I've seen women lose their husbands and I've seen men lose their fortunes, but nothing has brought me closer to losing my mind than the sight of my Geography mistress losing hers.

So people can say what they want and think what they like. Marconi Marsi was neither beast nor human. He was the Devil himself, building a bridgehead into the lives of innocent boys. And where did I recognise this truth? In the reflection in the eyes of the trusting beast I fed Marconi's sop.

Ψ

They didn't put you away for killing the dog, did they?

That was forty years ago, Stupid. But that was the beginning of my derailment. I managed to finish my final exams but I never went beyond secondary school. Marconi's kind of money was intoxicating. Within months I was filching from the markets. I was selling other people's goats. I was... well, you get the general idea. And I wasn't the only one too...

Was that why Madam-Put-More sacked you? Were you pocketing her money?

He peered suspiciously through the bars. For someone who knows nobody in town, you certainly know a lot about me. How did you know I worked for Madam-Put-More? That was thirty years ago.

Old woman told me, was the casual answer. So what are you doing here?

I killed a man by accident.

What?

He entered my restaurant four or five weeks ago. I was fourteen or so when he last saw me, but he was an adult and I recognised him immediately. The life of sin had not prospered him. He ordered stewed congo meat. He paused. I really stewed that meat, I tell you.

You poisoned Marconi Marsi?

I said it was an accident, he said impatiently. Just planned to give him a purge in revenge, you know. He must have had ulcers or something. He paused again. He did not sound very contrite when he added, He died painfully.

Somto paused. Are you going to hang for it?

Alfonso Etuna stretched. He opened a plastic plate by his bedside, speared a piece of fried snail meat with a toothpick and chewed nonchalantly: I've been cooking stewed congo for this town for twenty years without causing anybody even the smallest stomach ache. I won't even go to trial.

You won't?

This is Iria, not Lagos. This matter won't go beyond this station, you'll see. Marconi was an unknown drifter. I won't even be here at all if his companion hadn't filed a complaint here. He's gone now though. In another week it won't be scandalous to release me.

Somto paused, wondering that a forty-year old grudge had the sting to snuff out a very present life.

Alfonso Etuna paused and glared at Somto. And I'll do it all over again, if I had the chance... Look at me now! I could have been *anything!* Do you hear me? I could have been anything! he paused and took a deep breath before looking down at his hands. I could have been anything!

In the outer office, they heard the desk sergeant rise sleepily and cross over to the toilet. Through the open door, they listened to the water run. Then they listened to him resume his sleep. Remember that night? ventured Somto, That night that Madam PM sold the biggest meal ever in Iria?

Alfonso Etuna studied Somto through narrowed eyes. Sold is not the word... but how did you know about that mad man?

You're not the first to call him a mad man, said Somto evasively. He tensed. Did you ever see the Stranger again?

Alfonso laughed. He'll be dead by now. Starved or beaten to death, either one or the other.

Somto was silent for a long time. Etuna shifted impatiently. Go on, it's your turn now, pass the time.

Only story I know, you know it too.

Go on, give it another twist, tell your tale.

So Somto took a deep breath and retold *Silence in Heaven.*

When he was through Etuna stared at him with awe. By Iria! You actually resemble Madam PM!

Somto held his breath. Do I look like the mad man too?

Alfonso hesitated. Now, when I said mad man, I didn't really mean *mad*, you know... he fumbled in his pocket and pulled out Somto's watch. He crawled over and put it on the ground just inside the engineer's cell. He shrugged at Somto's quizzical look. I thought you were a money-miss-road engineer. Personally, I never take from the less fortunate. He rolled back under his blanket.

Where's Madam-Put-More now? Somto asked tersely.

Don't you mean her gravestone? asked Alfonso callously, watching Somto trying to play the man with mild amusement. You're better off looking for her daughter, should be a couple of years younger than you. She's called Madam-*Give*-More — behind her back! He laughed vulgarly. Listen, as far as stories go, that was some story, alright. But I don't know about all this rape business.

What?

What I mean is, food wasn't the Stranger's only weakness.

Although he was lying down, Somto began to feel giddy. He sat up carefully. What do you mean?

Alfonso laughed shortly. I don't know what happened that night he cut firewood for Madam PM – after all what goes on between a man and a woman is beyond the reach of investigative journalism. What I know is that he turned up the next day. And the day after. Look, he was a kind of celebrity at the buka. For the next few days till he continued his mad jouney, he had fools ready to buy him food.

Somto's mouth was dry. No, he disappeared the day after... He had... raped the Madam you see...

Alfonso coughed. Like I said, that was a powerful ending for a tale, but life is not a tale. You're talking to someone who was there, you see. You've told me some things I didn't know, I admit. *You* are a big surprise. Always thought Madam PM had just the one daughter. Always wondered where she disappeared to, that harmattan.

If it wasn't rape, mumbled Somto distractedly, why should she have abandoned me?

Alfonso Etuna reflected briefly and pronounced: Prestige. Tamar announced her pregnancy within a week of the Stranger's departure. Didn't know Madam PM was into the racket as well. The disgrace might have killed her. Explains why she never quite got along with Tamar thereafter. Obviously Madam PM couldn't bear to think she was carrying a baby for the same rascal that put her house-girl in the family way. He paused and coughed again. Women are such complicated people.

Something seemed to be caught in Somto's throat. It doesn't quite hang together, he hedged, he knew he had missed something, but he couldn't put a finger on it. He pressed on: The Stranger was on a mission to visit every town in the world.

Alfonso chuckled. Don't know about every town in the world, but he sure covered the neighbourhood. Tamar — and Madam PM — were not alone. He laughed raucously. You probably have brothers scattered all over the country!

Somto shut his eyes, silently burying the last hope of seeing his natural mother. By the time he was ready to ask after his half-sister, Alfonso Etuna had settled into a snore. He deliberately took his watch and buckled it on. From his pocket, he took out the remaining statement sheets left over from Inspector Vera's sheaf. His mother was dead and he'd never see Ma'Kanu again. Yet, in retelling *Silence in Heaven* to Etuna, he had been conscious of a blurring of detail: was it six wraps of pounded yam or *four* that his father had ordered? Was it a Chief Gbedu or *Gbaja* who ate under the canopy? He could no longer trust his memory with the harsher realities of his conception. He didn't want to go to sleep and wake up with the tale growing more palatable with each remembrance. Deliberately he wrote down the story of his paternity, recording every detail he could recall from Ma'Kanu's rendition.

He was roused the next morning by a kick in the side from a cursing desk sergeant, who cursed some more when his boot caught in the bars as he tried to yank it out of the cell. Somto rose. When he found his feet, he froze. His visitor was now dressed in a yellow slip shy of her knees, a black shawl was draped over her shoulder and a basket stood at her feet. It was the bride of the night before. Suddenly he didn't know whom he hated more, the bride or her groom.

As usual, his fury cost him his articulation. The sergeant shuffled back to his desk. Without uttering a word, he had left no one in any doubt about his opinion on the visit. Somto looked at the woman before him. In the stark light of the cell, she was a bland if arrogant woman, no longer the mysterious beauty of the night before. Or perhaps Somto was simply very angry. His first words, when they came, surprised him. Who are you?

I am still Elsie *Kunu*, if that is what you mean, I haven't married that thug yet. Shame on you, allowing fat Izzy to beat you up like that. Her actions didn't match her words and caught Somto by surprise. Before he realised what she was about, she had reached a slender hand through the bars to touch the bruises on his face. He slapped her hand away in a furious reflex and her wince was no playacting. She clicked her teeth, *Tut-tut,* a potential wife-beater!

Just get lost, okay,

I just came to say thank you.

What for.

For getting me out of my marriage.

I got you out of your marriage? *I* GOT YOU OUT OF YOUR MARRIAGE? He took a deep breath and began to pace the cell. Even in his frustration, he could feel the tension from the huddle in the other cell as Alfonso pretended to be fast asleep. The Sergeant walked in and warned: Two minutes more.

Elsie only laughed derisively. When he had gone, she said in a low voice, I think I should tell you the truth…

I think you had better, he snapped and she paused, amused.

She regarded him speculatively. And what are you going to do if I don't? He realized, with dismay, that there in the middle of the savanna he had stumbled upon the tease to end all teases.

He remained silent and she pouted, I think I've changed my mind. Even Izzy never treated me so callously. I brought you breakfast and the thanks I get is to be slapped *and kicked around.*

Slapped and kicked around? Get yourself and your stupid breakfast out of here! Sergeant!

She pushed the basket closer to his cell. So my food has now become stupid? Well, let me warn you that the woman who cooks for the police station has tuberculosis. One day very soon you'll wish you ate your girlfriend's stupid breakfast instead.

She swept around as the Sergeant entered. I've come to bail my boyfriend, she announced grandly, fill out the form for me to sign. What has he done that he should sleep in the cell when there are so many empty beds in my father's house? Somto looked on impotently, lost for words.

He thought he was beyond surprises when Sergeant Vera pushed the door open and snapped, his face even stonier than it was the night before when he arrested Somto in his small hotel, Just forget about bail, you hear me? We've found Izoun.

Where was he hiding, demanded Somto uncomprehendingly, and what does it have to do with my bail?

We found him floating in the river where you left him; and there's no police bail in murder cases.

Elsie's mouth dropped open. She did not speak another word and was out of the station with her basket within the minute.

Things started moving very fast after that. Alfonso Etuna woke up with a mournful expression. He would not meet Somto's eyes and presaged every comment with a tragic sigh. Outside the police station, a hubbub began to build until, within the hour, the chanting of a full-scale riot could be heard. The desk Sergeant opened the cell and pushed in a tin plate of beans. Better eat, he said unsympathetically. It's unfair to be lynched on an empty stomach. Famished though he was, Somto didn't stir towards the food. He sat on the cold floor of the cell, in a kind of daze, listening to the rioters and trying to persuade himself that they were not screaming for his blood.

What's happening to me? whispered Somto.

Thinking as a crook, said Alfonso, I'd say you were in the wrong place at the wrong time. Izoun may be an ugly beast, but he's one rich animal. He paid the biggest dowry in Iria's history.

What's that got to do with me?

By Iria tradition, if Elsie calls off the wedding, she's got to refund the dowry. But if she can get Izoun to call it off — provoked by jealousy or rage — she gets to keep it.

But she knew my name.

She likely saw you with your friend Moonshine. Couldn't have cost her more than a beer or two. You were her fall guy; but you weren't meant to kill poor Izoun.

I...

An intent look entered Alfonso's eyes and he put a finger on his lips and pointed at the passage that led to the front office. Somto listened. Despite the noise of the mob it was possible to hear the policemen quarrelling. The mob was threatening to burn down the station and not all the policemen were keen on martyrdom just to have Somto executed a few months later by due process of law. The only voice on the side of duty seemed to be Inspector Vera's, but discipline within the Police Force seemed in clear and apparent danger of meltdown. Somto tried to focus his mind with an effort. You've got to help me, Alfonso, These cops have finished their investigations. Tell me, who could possibly want Izoun dead in this town?

You mean apart from you?

Somto hesitated then he started to his feet and lunged at the bars separating him from the other man. That woman is crazy! I tell you, I've nothing to do with this matter!

Neither do I, said Alfonso truculently, and I'm certainly not going to burn by accident. He got to his feet and banged on his own cell door. Inspector Vera! *Inspector Vera!*

Suddenly, there was a sharp crack as Inspector Vera fired his side arm into the air; and there was silence, not just in the police station but all around. Out in the Incident Room, Inspector Vera reholstered his revolver angrily, thinking of the hour-and-a-half of form-filling he had triggered by that single bullet. A moment later, three loud retorts came from the rioters as they discharged throaty double-barrels into the air.

The chanting resumed in force.

Moments later, Inspector Vera came in with a riot police helmet and a bundle of clothes. He engaged Somto's door and in a trice the cell door stood open. He dumped the bundle on the floor of the cell and snapped. Get that on top of your clothes, quick.

Hey Inspector, yelled Alfonso, what about me?

You aren't the one they want to fry, grated Inspector Vera as Somto struggled into a creased police uniform. He fumbled with the outsized belt until Vera snarled and hooked it up for him.

Are you crazy? yelped Alfonso Etuna. Those people are going to burn this place down.

Vera paused. Then he turned to Alfonso. If my detainee is lynched inside my own cell, the paperwork could cost me my pension. I'm transferring him right now to the divisional headquarters in Kebbi. By Monday his case will be in the High Court. You still want to join him?

Alfonso took a deep breath. He turned away. His voice snarled with a false bravura, These are my people. They won't harm me.

I thought so, muttered Inspector Vera. He grabbed Somto by the arm and pulled him out. Roughly, he set the helmet on his head, then he rapped the barrel of the revolver against the tinted visor of the helmet. It's not bullet proof, he cautioned. Don't get ideas, an escapee's shooting is easier to explain than a detainee's lynching.

Three scowling policemen stood around the counter in the station's incident room, Two others manned the main doors, which had been barred against the crowd. As a revolver-waving Vera squeezed past them with two other policemen in riot gear, the raging villagers hurling expletives at them. They made it to the car. Somto had never been the subject of so much odium; or been in such manifest physical danger. As he sat there waiting for the backfiring engine to catch, he had to exercise the ultimate personal discipline not to bolt from the car and take to his heels.

Eventually, they took off and rattled down the road away from the station. The Iria Police station was tucked away behind the town cinema. Inspector Vera careered away from the close and took off down the Main Road towards Madam-Put-More's. Whoa! yelled Somto, You're going the wrong way, the pontoon's that way.

You didn't recognise the Mariner back there? asked Inspector Vera tersely, He was the one that found Izoun's corpse and he's at the head of your lynch mob at the station.

Somto didn't say another word as Inspector Vera ran his car recklessly through the small town. Within ten minutes he slowed down as he pulled into a gloomy neighbourhood with a column of citrus trees down both sides. The street itself was a series of great puddles in and out of which the car rolled. It paused on the lip of another puddle and Inspector Vera switched off the engine.

Now let me tell you, he said severely, passing the station's only revolver to the man in the back with Somto, I'm protecting my pension, not your life. If you try to escape, Pitam will put a bullet in your leg and leave you for the mob to finish up. — And then you will know that a state execution is mercy killing compared to what I've just saved you from.

I take it you have finished your investigation.

I might think of resuming it when you're ready to make a new statement. Inspector Vera cranked the ignition, which obliged immediately. Somto stepped down with his silent minder.

Where are you taking me now?

The policeman indicated a small house behind the screen of citrus. A place where nobody will think of looking for you. With that he rolled into the next stagnant pool. The two men in riot gear picked their way onto the grass verge and thence into a modest, red-brick property. The front door was standing open a crack and when they stepped up, a woman in gray brocade pulled it open with her left hand. Her right hand was encased in an oily glove and the pleasant aroma of fried plantain chips hit them from the door. Her eyes were wary and unfriendly and her lips sealed in an uncompromising line.

Good day, Coffey, said the policeman. The woman made a neutral sound in her throat as she locked the door behind them. They stood in a pokey living room with several doors opening out of it. Three cushion chairs were arranged in a semi circle, away from a huge basket of fried plantain chips and a bean bag. She gestured towards the chairs without a word as she sank onto the bean bag and tackled the packing of the chips into polythene bags. In the eerie silence that followed, the policeman repossessed the riot police gear that got Somto out of the clutches of the lynch mob. Then his eyes lit up as they fell on a pack of cards on a coffee table. He stripped off his jacket, lifted off his own helmet and placed Inspector Vera's revolver into it.

Come, he said, breaking the deck gleefully, my hundred naira says you'll mess up this one as well.

I haven't got a hundred naira, said Somto, staring at the plantain chips with longing.

The deputy's quick eyes frisked Somto professionally. Okay, we'll play for fifty. I'm sure your watch is worth that at least.

Pitam! said Coffey, in a voice that was three-quarters amazement and one-quarter disapproval.

He doesn't need a watch where he's going! protested the policeman.

After three games, the deputy was wearing Somto's watch and gold chain. The game seemed to degenerate into a strip poker as Somto lost his boots and baseball cap. Coffey's monosyllables and throaty sighs grew more disapproving in tone, until she rose and fetched a bottle of a local brew from one of the adjoining rooms. The deputy whooped as Somto lost his belt. He whooped again when he saw the bottle and thanked the taciturn Coffey effusively. He filled a glass and took a gulp before offering it to his victim. At first Somto declined, but the deputy's scowl prompted him to take a tiny sip, which burnt away the linings of his mouth. The policeman roared in laughter and took another mouthful.

Pitam didn't win another game. His coordination spiralled downhill after that. Slowly, Somto got dressed again. Just before he won back his watch, the deputy stretched luxuriantly and fell asleep. Somto stared slack-jawed, stunned at the suddenness of his opponent's retirement. He looked at the woman. What did you put in the drink?

Nothing, she said. Her voice was low and deeply accented. It's our traditional firewater, but everyone knows Pitam's weakness, except Pitam. She paused briefly. What are you waiting for?

Eh?

Aren't you going to escape?

They'll kill me if I step out that door.

Use the backdoor. – Because they'll kill you if you stay here. Vera likes to deceive himself, but everyone in Iria knows I'm his girlfriend.

He stood up uncertainly. Pitam woke up with a start, but his wide eyes were unseeing, and he merely settled into a more comfortable position. Inspector Vera will kill you, he ventured.

She smiled and stuck her little finger in the air. I can turn the big inspector around this little finger. She took two packets of plantain chips from the basket and threw them at Somto with a grin. *This is why you couldn't concentrate on your card games! Don't eat them too quickly, there's no shop for the next thirty miles until you get to Tonga. Just go through my back door, turn left, and follow the river. Those orange overalls! You have to crawl for the first two hundred metres till you're clear of the village. After that... I'm sure you can run the race of life as fast as anyone else.*

Somto hesitated. He couldn't credit the turn of events, or the fact that he was about to leave his hometown for what had better be the last time. As he stepped across the room, he tried to understand her bewildering kindness, *Why are you doing this?*

She laughed as an asthmatic car wheezed to a standstill in front of the house. Her laughter went with her voice, low, husky and self-possessed. *You're very slow today, mister. I'm only helping you because Izoun left here drunk and frustrated yesterday night. Don't know what gave him the impression that I was the Balm of Jilted Husbands. I guess that's what comes of a nickname like Madam-Give-More. Anyway, the pontoon had closed for the night, but he decided to try his luck at the truck-stop across the river.* She shook her head. *The Kigalo can be an ocean when you're drunk. I know you're innocent of his murder, mister, but I'll never say it aloud. Vera may be a baby with me, but jealousy turns him into a tiger...*

He looked from her to the photograph of a severe, matronly type on the wall. His mouth was open and incredulous. *Madam PM was your mother?*

She looked at him with some perplexity. On the street, a car door slammed. *You're a strange one, aren't you. That's Vera coming. I could tell him I saw you turn* right *at the river as I came out of the toilet, but that won't help you if you're still looking at my family album when he enters.*

Somto shook himself out of his stupor. Fate was consistently capricious, but at least it was not consistently contrary. He grabbed her hand. He tried to rein in his feelings, but... *was this his blood?* Without thinking, he was unstrapping her watch, squeezing her hand reassuringly. *I need a watch but I can't risk waking Pitam for mine.*

Her watch was in his pocket before she could react, and he could not help reflecting that Alfonso's watch trick was certainly catching. He snatched the wad of pages that retold *Silence in Heaven* from an inner pocket and squeezed them into her hands as he took two steps backwards, Read it, Coffey, I'm the child on the last page.

What's this? she asked without comprehension, opening the pouch he had secreted among the papers.

Keep it. He said without hesitation. Then he was inside a warm kitchen. The suddenly ubiquitous face of Madam-Put-More glared, appropriately, from above the cooker. Without thinking, he snatched the small frame and went through a mosquito-gauze screen running, doubled up, for the bushes that fringed the Kigalo.

*

The arrival of Somto's jeep did not exactly cause a stir at Grace Lodge. Kanu's empty car stood in front of the gate in the middle of a profusion of bicycles and motorcycles. A dozen villagers loitered on the veranda. No one moved to acknowledge him, and that was just as well, for his face seemed cut from a block of flint, no good for the Saint's usually courteous smiles.

The crowded house spoke volumes and he knew she was dead. In a vain search for the mother he never knew, the only one he did know had died behind his back. He might as well have stayed back on the rig. He was motionless for a good half hour, trying to rationalise his presence at Grace Lodge to himself, without success. The fury that propelled him from Grace House hours earlier had quite evaporated. What was left was a clumsy ambivalence. So she had told a tale out of turn. So what? As he picked at the worn leather strips on his steering wheel, he felt childish and ineffectual, beginning to envy Ma'Kanu the ability to nurse a grudge decisively for decades at a stretch. Then Kanu and Udeme appeared from the direction of Ekwutosia's Provision Store; Kanu smiled when he recognised Somto's jeep.

The way you left, said Kanu as they shook hands, I didn't think you were coming back this year.

Somto shrugged defiantly. I didn't think I'd meet you here either!

Kanu jerked a thumb at Ezinne who had suddenly bustled onto the veranda from the house, her progress impeded by commiserating villagers. He complained, a tad sheepishly, She seized my keys!

The edge of grief had gone, he recognised that much, as he watched Ezinne... then he looked at Udeme again. *She* had not cracked a smile — and she held his eyes in an unfriendly gaze. What's the matter, Udeme?

She doesn't remember your begging visit quite the way you described it in *The Day of the Jewel*, replied Kanu tautly.

What? gaped Somto.

She doesn't remember offering you any of our children. She doesn't remember all the dramatics of fluttering notes and prayer altars... and *I* certainly don't appreciate my wife being described as a widower. I was only on a trip when you came begging for money.

Somto took a deep breath. How did you hear the story?

Ezinne retold all the stories we missed, said Udeme. She paused significantly, Yours was very entertaining, *Tikum*.

Somto groaned as Ezinne extricated herself from the veranda and began to walk across the garden. He whispered urgently, Does she know... everything?

Not yet, said Udeme tersely, and you have only until after Ma is buried to tell them what's true and what's a tale — or else...

And you're going to tell us the *whole* truth this time Somto, warned Kalu, I'm sick and tired of secrets in this family.

Ezinne arrived at the jeep, a teenager in a woman's body, and Somto hugged her stiffly. When did she die? he asked.

Yesterday, Ezinne replied. She's at peace now.

Njide appeared on the veranda herself, with a lot more dignity, carrying Ma'Kanu's purple bundle in her arms. They watched her approach, with a lot more reserve than was her wont, in the careful minefield of their post-Ma'Kanu world. Welcome home, Somto, she said with a forced smile.

I have a confession to make, he replied in a monotone, I'm the Tikum in *The Day of the Jewel*. Jorie was my wife Getty – and the jewels kept her home for less than a fortnight. She had her fatal heart attack in a lover's bed ten days after I brought the jewels home...

You, Tikum? marvelled Ezinne. He was married to Jorie for ages!

I changed a few things for Ma'Kanu's benefit. — I was married to Getty for twelve months, not twelve years, it all happened in New Bussa, not Potiskum... and I couldn't keep her at home...

Aw, murmured Udeme softly into the stunned silence. She dispensing a hug from the rear, there are girls like that, hairpins that won't be straightened out, ever. It wasn't your fault.

Slowly, the moment of nakedness passed. Akin to the shock that followed the telling of *Silence in Heaven*, it was nowhere near as acute. Kanu clapped him clumsily on the shoulder and slowly, Somto began to know the relief of a family in whose eyes saintly airs were redundant.

You're even more secretive than Ma! said Njide undiplomatically.

Somto managed a smile, What d'you expect? It's a gene thing.

And Nne? asked Ezinne mischievously, did you go back to her?

Somto clutched his chest where he had taken Nne's finger and staggered against his jeep. Njide was the only one who wasn't laughing. Kanu stared at the bundle in her hands, What's that?

Ma's bundle. She wanted it buried with her, but she made me promise not to open it.

Kanu hesitated. He had no real desire to open the bundle. All he meant was some horseplay with Njide, a sort of circuitous apology for his earlier coldness, which had not survived an encounter with Ezinne's deprecative wit. He reached for the bundle. Well, *I* didn't.

Njide made a stagey attempt to get away, succeeding only in spilling the contents of the bundle on the ground. The Bible was expected, amongst the poignant spill of colour that was Ma'Kanu's deck of story cards. The small, glass-framed wedding photograph broke and Kanu gasped. He had never before seen an image of his father; or a photograph of his mother that young. The wedding ring was also somewhat of a surprise, for they'd never seen it before. Ezinne kicked out her foot, irritably, to stop it rolling into a puddle. It occurred to her that death's cruellest cut was the stripping away of the very last veil of privacy, especially when all one left behind were irreverent children.

She picked up the ring, and then the Bible. A picture of a teen-age Udeme slipped out of the book. Udeme gasped and snatched at it. Then she took the Bible gently from Ezinne and opened it with trembling hands. She smelt her flower before she saw it, the white and orange glory of it pressed into Psalm 32. There was one more picture inside. Weeping, she turned it so Kanu could see. Ezinne stood up disconcerted, glancing from Somto to a quiet Njide. I don't understand, she tore the last picture of them that we showed her... why should she salt away these ones to be buried with?

'Cos she's a rotten liar, whispered Njide.

And a proud and stubborn old dear, sobbed Udeme, her arms around her husband's neck. K, she gave you all her stubbornness.

After an age, conscious of the brace of chattering children gathering, Kanu pulled gently apart from his wife. Not quite all of it, he heaved eventually. He looked from the overgrown hedges and the over-enthusiastic sprays to Somto who was already rolling his sleeves. He nodded approvingly. Let's go bury the old coot.

As they moved resolutely into Grace Lodge, Njide hung back, humming as she made up Ma'Kanu's bundle again under Ezinne's puzzled eyes. She looked up, and misunderstood the expression in her sister's eyes: Don't worry, I've always wanted the Bible, but I'm not going to *steal* from the dead!

*

In the evening they gathered to put the shawled body down the grave. It was an unusual graveside, the exigencies of the freshly trimmed hedges had the villagers lining up in strange lines and circles in the maze of flowers. Mother Clementina was uncharacteristically late and none of the children of Grace House felt up to the lengthy oration required to keep her place in the programme. After your shameful behaviour, said Njide, into a suddenly thunderous silence, my mother didn't want any of you here. Then she smiled to take the edge off her words. But I know one apology Ma could never resist.

There was a stir of interest but no takers. For it had to be a superlative story if it was expected to atone for the sins of Odozi — and serenade the storyteller herself. Udeme felt the wave of anticipation spread in the garden, and she remembered how, back when they were children, adults always seemed to time their visits to either begin or end in the evenings so they could sit in, accidentally, on Ma'Kanu's story circle.

Eventually, Givemore coughed and made his way closer to the bank of pink roses. To make the story a decent length, Kanu fetched a stool for him and planted it beside Ma'Kanu's body. Givemore sighed gratefully as he stretched out his unsteady legs. He leaned forward and patted the head of the corpse reverently. It was an oddly touching gesture from a man that the whole of Odozi considered to be Ma'Kanu's unrequited suitor.

You always had a big heart Cecelia, he began, and no one could tell a tale better than you. Well, you're speechless now, and I may stammer a little but you're just going to have to be patient, aren't you? He turned to the villagers of Odozi. I'm going to tell a story about another funeral. A funeral in a town called Keyside. It's a little bit true and a little bit tall. He shrugged. I can feel the story coming.

I can feel two itching ears! came the resounding boom.

THE EVIDENCE
OF THE STEW

$$\Psi$$

Although Neze's country home in the sleepy village of Keyside had been under construction for almost eight years, one would never have thought so, to see the house, which was still no taller than a man. It wasn't the grandness of the master plan that crippled construction, much less the absence of funds for the project; for no Keysider had a more successful enterprise than Neze's Serene Canteen in Lagos. If anyone could afford to build a five-bedroom detached house in his own hometown, Neze could.

Unfortunately, every time the talented cook arrived at Keyside with his savings, he invariably paused for a chinwag and a plate of pepper soup at Comfort's buka. By the time he finally arrived at the decrepit bungalow he'd inherited from his father, it was usually in the company of needy villagers trying to provoke his inveterate compassion into irresponsible charity. He was such a soft touch that his ne'er-do-well brother no longer bothered to make personal appearances: Paddy's creditors brought his latest credit notes directly to Neze for settlement.

Keysiders were practised beggars, although they didn't look the part at first blush. However tragic their faces, their bodies were plump, verging on the gross. They arrived well-dressed, with over-ripe avocados, a basket of oranges and similar thoughtful edibles with which to welcome their illustrious son who had made good in Lagos. They were also a proud people, but hours into their long visits (in the course of which they invariably consumed their own gifts) their desperate needs usually reduced them — and the sentimental Neze as well — to tears.

Margarita for instance always carried her latest suspension slips with her. She was a distant relative of Neze's, but in Keyside that wasn't saying much, for with a population of five thousand and a culture of intermarriage, many people had one blood relationship or the other. She'd had seven inadvertent kids for as many clients. All her children were still in school — but for the eldest girl who was working at Comfort's buka while awaiting her GCE results. Although the light-skinned Margarita had recently retired from the entertainment business, she didn't draw a pension and one or more of her children were usually out of school for unpaid bills. She'd sit silently, with a tragic, tight-lipped air, until Neze was compelled to inquire what the problem was.

He found it impossible to deny his hometown folk.

Even with Ezeta, an old teammate on the Keyside Eleven, it was dangerous merely to ask 'how are things'? That was invitation enough to be brought up-to-date with the latest tragedy in the ironmonger's life. As lives went, Ezeta's didn't seem that tragic, but the former centre-forward had a knack for putting a calamitous spin on everything. He seemed a successful ironmonger; for instance he'd only recently moved into his own brand-new house. On paper that ranked him somewhat above Neze in status, but by the time a distraught Ezeta explained the rising price of steel, his banker's foreclosure threat and how his ex-wife had turned his bank account into an excavation site — before eloping with his foreman, Neze felt obligated to advance the substantial loan that would clear the mortgage arrears on the ironmonger's bungalow.

Neze's presence caused Keysiders to degenerate into grievous sighs and long faces — all of which disappeared as the sympathetic cook unzipped his money belt. By dawn, when he approached his construction site, it was usually with a failing heart and a flat belt. He was never able to do much beyond hiring a labourer to clear the rampaging bushes and add a dozen blocks or so to the building-in-progress.

His wife was of a different mould altogether. Keyside folk never figured out how a man as open-handed as Neze ended up with a woman as tight-fisted as Casca. Her mind functioned like digital equipment on which sentimental issues simply didn't register. Yet, she had no particular talent — unless the management of a spendthrift husband was a talent, in which case she was probably deserving of a professorship. Before they met on the eve of Neze's 40th birthday, Neze had been on starvation wages with a Lagos restaurateur, who prevented his workers from resigning by keeping their salaries two to three months in arrears. He lived in a garret and endured all manner of insults from his landlady on account of his perpetually late rent.

Casca had never considered herself a poor cook until she met the man who was later to become her husband. The first time she tasted his beef stew, she'd overeaten massively. She'd spent a painful night rolling on her bed, muttering 'Witchcraft!' over and over. Thereafter she was ruined for her own cooking. Within weeks of their first meeting, Casca, ten years his junior, determined that they should get married. She also decided he should leave his job and start a canteen in his landlady's disused garage. Neze's obliging character didn't permit him to deny friends presumptuous enough to ask anything, even when their requests pertained to matters as fundamental as matrimony and career. He usually depended on the impossibility of the requests to maintain his status quo.

Casca overwhelmed him.

Her name meant nothing, being the careless misspelling of a UNHCR official. She was the stateless daughter of a Somalian refugee who was in-between countries when he was clubbed to death for stealing fruits at a local market. She was a foster child of the largest civil service in the world and the life-and-death desperation she brought to her undertakings sapped the will of those who crossed her path.

Neze's impossible landlady found Casca equally impossible to refuse and the laid-back cook had watched with a kind of fascination as the garage was emptied and cleared even before a rent was agreed or paid. The day after he said 'Let's see how it goes' to her wedding proposal, Neze arrived at work to discover that Casca had resigned for him. She'd also snapped the salary arrears chain by confiscating a box of silver cutlery worth more than his four months' wages. He returned home, not exactly vexed, to find grumbling workmen fitting out an oven for him on credit.

He married her before she developed second thoughts.

Serene Canteen opened. He was a gifted cook and conversationalist; and she was a ruthless manager of man and resources. The landlady, who didn't know what she'd let herself in for, couldn't bear the heat of the oven — or the racket of patrons who kept trooping into her premises well after dark. She allowed herself to be bought out within the year and Serene Canteen ballooned into the main house. Neze woke 4 am daily, including Sundays. He toiled in the kitchen till 7 am when Casca opened the doors of a not-so-serene canteen. He then stripped his gloves to lounge with his patrons, whom he delighted with rib-cracking jokes till they closed at 6 pm.

Neze's conversation was an art form. As between the food and the talk it was impossible to tell what brought more people to Serene. Because of the pressure for seats, customers sometimes dallied over a final spoonful for the half-hour it took a particular yarn to run its addictive course — yet, there wasn't a single day that another glutton didn't howl in pain as he chewed his tongue along with Neze's luscious beef. During the Easter Jollof Night, a wounded customer swore that Neze's beef stew ought to carry a Ministry of Health warning like less pernicious cigarettes.

Casca manned the cash register in the canteen. She was as brusque as her husband was engaging. Even those customers who had been lunching at *Serene* for a decade didn't qualify for credit in her books. The best an apologetic Neze could do for indignant customers was to slip some extra hot water past Casca to augment their pots of tea.

They prospered.

Sour grapes would say that Casca was too business-minded to conceive, but the absence of children didn't seem to bother Neze. Indeed it was difficult to imagine anything that could bother the genial cook. Even when he returned from his abortive building campaigns to Keyside and Casca raged at the dissipation of their hard-won funds, he'd only shrug: 'Better to mould cassava blocks in somebody's stomach than cement blocks for *Serene Lodge!*'

On that eighth anniversary of the foundations of their Keyside house, she could bear it no longer. The housing loan to Ezeta was particularly riling, coming from a Neze whose current family house was a century-old mud hut. She resolved to risk one week's takings in order to safeguard their savings from months of hard work: she left the running of the restaurant to Neze and undertook the week-long trip to Keyside.

She'd initially opposed the Keyside project, thinking it madness to build an expensive house — which would be empty most of year — in a village with abysmal real estate values. Yet a country home in his beloved Keyside was a project of such passionate significance to the cook that his wife had gracefully yielded. By that night when she arrived at Keyside, she'd lost all her reservations on the project. She went straight to the old house to sleep but by morning the news of her arrival had spread, for Keyside was that sort of place. Courtesy callers swamped the cook's wife. She received them over breakfast, listening politely to their convoluted appeals for assistance.

A red-eyed Ezeta was there, with a decree nisi in one hand and a court order for repossession in the other, but the only person who got anything out of her could hardly be called a person, being the dog that nosed through the parsimonious scraps of her breakfast. Within an hour of waking up, she was off to the building site where she spent most of the next week. It was there that Keysiders got to relieve Casca of her money, by hiring their labour to her for wages and earning razor-thin profits from selling supplies to the shrewdest builder that ever laid brick on brick in Keyside. All day and all week, she was buying bags of cement, tipper-loads of sharp sand, headpans of gravel and roofing sheets. Even Ezeta was procured to deliver tons of nails and iron rods; although when it was time to pay him, she shook out her empty purse and asked him to take it out of the over-due loan he owed her husband. She'd left for Lagos before he recovered his voice.

Neze couldn't quarrel with the progress of the house and he never made another visit to the village — until the visit in the course of which he died. The house was completed a few months after Casca took it personally in hand. Being just a five-room house, it wasn't exactly the largest residence in Keyside. On account of his harem, Chief Banjo's palace had almost a dozen rooms; but it was more warren-like than palatial. Neze's well-appointed house on the other hand was built on four levels, with a fenced-in lawn larger than the village's community centre. Beyond sheer size, Casca had brought a design-savvy into the finish of the house that incited neighbours into painting and varnishing their own facades to reduce the aesthetic gulf between the new house and the rest of Keyside. Casca was sufficiently proud of her achievement to do something completely out of character: she suggested a housewarming feast.

Neze's death itself was one of those thoroughly baffling events life threw up time and again. It happened on the eve of the housewarming. The cakes had been baked. The yams, peeled and chopped, were soaking in basins, waiting for the morrow to be boiled and pounded. In the backyard grew a soggy mound of chicken feathers whose dismembered owners marinated in earthenware pots. Night fell. Neze and Casca were in bed for the night when he remembered a promise to deliver a pot of Jollof rice to the Covent school. It was 10 pm, and she blew some fuses. But without raising his voice, the easy-going Neze could be stubborn in his generosities. Their pick-up fired into life. Fifteen minutes later, it was still idling in the drive and a repentant Casca walked downstairs to urge him on. The cook was slumped in the driver's seat, wearing the puzzled frown with which he confronted eternity.

The next morning, Casca insisted that the housewarming continue in the capacity of a funeral feast. It was a decision that reflected amazing presence of mind, saved her a tidy sum, and had unfortunate reverberations months into the future. The reverend who had been ancillary to the scheduled event suddenly became central to the impromptu one, but he rose handsomely to the occasion. Casca pointed out a spot in the middle of the lawn for Neze's grave. Despite the macabre turn the housewarming had taken, she maintained her composure, nodding sadly at the significant cusp when Neze disappeared underground. She then requested Chief Banjo, who had just arrived, to unveiled the plaque that christened the house 'Serene Lodge'.

All of which did her reputation no good. Of course, indignant Keysiders had no way of telling that culturally, her nod was the equivalent of their shake of the head — or that her tear-ducts had last functioned, age ten, when she survived the gang-rape by rebels that left her mother and sisters dead.

Within days, she'd put her marriage behind her, shut up the house, and resumed the management of the Lagos canteen. She hired the best cook she could find, and, to avoid too funereal an atmosphere, took to wearing gray rather than black behind the cash register. She struggled for one month but it simply wasn't working. The business haemorrhaged cash. It wasn't just that the quality of the food had crashed, which it had, or that the canteen lacked a foil for the commercial fire of Casca's presence behind the cash machine, which it did. The core problem was that the canteen's regulars resented Casca's cavalier handling of them like mere gullets equipped with wallets. They had voted with their feet. Nightly, Serene Canteen grew more and more serene. The few loyal customers talked perpetually about Neze. The canteen was steeped in the despondency of a wake, which, aside from scaring off new custom was inimical to digestion.

One night, the canteen's auditor interrupted a heated quarrel between Casca and the third cook since Neze's demise. His black bag produced, first a red-streaked analysis sheet, then a terse offer from a buyer. It didn't take long to persuade Casca that the canteen would fetch more as a going-concern than as bric-a-brac in a boot sale.

Casca sold.

The failure of the business, so soon after Neze's death, destroyed her. She'd always known that the business would have gone bust within a month of her predeceasing Neze. She had never dreamt that the converse was true as well. She'd weathered the loss of her family and her spouse. She'd survived the loss of her innocence as a child, but it was the loss of her pride as an adult that spun her into a severe midlife crisis. Yet, with the proceeds from the canteen's sale, she could afford to indulge depression. She slunk home to Keyside and pulled the gates of her hermitage shut after her.

If the truth be told, Keyside wasn't near the top of her list of venues for a hermitage. Yet the riverside village was so isolated that the only possible buyers of Serene Lodge were the residents of the village, none of whom could have paid for the house, even if it were auctioned at a tenth of its value. Although she had nothing in common with the villagers, Serene Lodge was the only root she had, anywhere in the world. She lived a quiet, self-sufficient life, aloof from the villagers, doing her shopping in nocturnal drives to Benin.

However, if she succeeded in putting the villagers out of her mind, she remained uppermost in theirs. On a daily basis, She was the subject of simultaneous conversations around Keyside. Serene Canteen was the

'Crown Jewel' of Keyside and the news of its sale swept Keyside like a tsunami, provoking a rash of gossip in the village. The jigsaw puzzle of Neze's life came together in a popular picture that fired Keyside's collective indignation. Chief Banjo considered himself above gossip, but he had little control over the sessions that took place in his lounge, especially after his guests had indulged his potent akpeteshi brew.

'She got him cheap.'

'Dirt cheap.'

'She ought to be arrested! Are there elders in this village or what?'

'But there's no evidence, only supposition...'

'Suppo? Suppo-what? A woman has the effrontery to organise her husband's burial feast even before murdering him and you're still suppositing. No, it's not supposition, call it suppository!'

'I'm not siding her; I'm just talking about evidence that can stand up in court.'

'Come and help me hear nonsense! The house Neze was building for years, Delilah nags him to finish it overnight; she kills him the day it is painted, she buries him the very next day — then she auctions his business, the biggest canteen in Lagos — and this emergency-lawyer is still waiting for evidence to stand up and dance for him!'

'That's true. When I heard that she was doing housewarming, I went to buy cotton-buds for my ears — to hear better. Because nobody has ever eaten Casca's free rice before, and I was right.'

'And did you hear her shouting curses, the very night she killed him?'

'And did you see her nodding when Neze entered the ground?'

'And did you see her eyes, dry like a witch's own? Have you ever seen a woman bury her husband without crying?'

'Her own witchcraft is wearing high heels, true.'

'But does everything have to be witchcraft? You know she's a foreigner. Maybe in her country they don't cry to bury their husbands.'

'Me, I've travelled my own share of travelling and I've never seen people who bleed oil — or widows who don't cry water. She's a witch, true.'

'Superstitious monkeys! Does everything have to be witchcraft?'

'That's true; it may be ordinary wickedness. She could have used rat poison.'

*

The most vexed issue was the inheritance of Serene Lodge: clearly, after her heinous crime, Casca didn't have long to live. Already Keysiders were speaking of her in the past tense. Had she been anyone else's widow, she could have enjoyed her spoils in security; but there wasn't a soul in all Keyside who wasn't a beneficiary of Neze's kindness. One night very soon, someone was going to stick a hypodermic of rat poison into a pawpaw and make her a gift.

As Neze's closest relative, Paddy's life was about to be transformed. With a History degree, he was better educated than Neze, but he had never served a full month's employment in his life. It was probably the sheer injustice of the situation that had so far stayed the hands of the numerous vigilante killers waiting in the wings: the fact that the laziest villager in Keyside was about to come into such a stupendous inheritance. Keysiders watched the house every night, sighing each time the lights winked on.

Two Keysiders, for their own different reasons, didn't particularly care whether Casca was a murderess or not.

Ezeta was one of them. Soon after Casca's retirement to Keyside, he'd bought a new courting suit, an all-white affair, and visited Neze's widow. At first, like every other villager, he couldn't make it through her gate. He had returned home thoughtfully, wrote a cheque for the balance of Neze's loan, and put it in the post. He gave it one week and donned his new suit again. That Saturday, he made it through the gate, on the first of what was to become his regular weekend visits. That same Saturday, Paddy's credit line at Comfort's Buka and HiLife Convenience Stores dried up. — And Keysiders began to speculate on the prospects of a supervening wedding before the funeral.

What Ezeta didn't disclose was that he paid his visits standing on the patch of lawn between the gate and the kitchen door. Keysiders would also have been shocked to learn that he'd managed to establish the Saturday visits to start with, by causing his cheque to bounce and contriving to pay the outstanding balance in mincing weekly instalments. So far, every personal twist to the visits had been firmly repulsed by Casca. He'd compliment the lawn and the garden and her dress. He'd produce an album of his last visit to Yankari Game Reserves, which was best viewed sitting down... but once her money was in her hand, she was walking towards the gate to let him out. As between Paddy and the ironmonger, most Keysiders were rooting for Ezeta, but he also knew he was running out of time.

Margarita was the other person. When she got the bad news from Dr Joda, Casca's house was the last of the seven homes at which she called. That Monday, eight weeks after her retirement to Keyside, Casca had cooked breakfast as usual. Covering it up, she'd glumly walked her grounds for an hour in search of an appetite. Finally she returned to the kitchen, opened her plate of pap and began to eat with all the enjoyment of one that drank a medicine.

Suddenly, a frantic banging was unleashed on her gates. She was alarmed, in spite of herself, and swung the pedestrian entrance open, totally unprepared for the sight of a nervously grinning Margarita and her eldest daughter. Margarita managed to slip through before Casca recovered her indignation and slammed the gate shut against the hesitant teenager shifting from foot to foot. The widow wheeled furiously on Margarita. 'How dare you bang my gates like that?'

The other woman shrugged. 'You'll never know why, till I tell you — and I never talk standing up. Let my girl come in and wait in your garden, what I have to say is for your ears only.'

Her presumption was exactly what was required. After eight weeks, Casca was sick of her own company; but she wasn't exactly about to go out and solicit visitors. She knew that whatever Margarita wanted would fit into a begging bowl. She normally had one short answer for all beggars, but right then she wasn't averse to saying 'No' more elaborately. She let the girl into the garden and led Margarita into her kitchen.

Margarita gaped at the food on the table. 'That's not your breakfast!'

'I'm not hungry,' snapped Casca, dreading the gossip the plate of pap would spawn, and beginning to regret letting Margarita in. '— and it's none of your business anyway. What do you want?'

'I've some lovely pumpkins ripening in my...'

'I'm not hungry...' insisted Casca, peeved at the pity in Margarita's eyes.

'They're going to waste anyway, besides pumpkins go well with pap.' Margarita hurried into the garden and Casca turned her scowl to her breakfast. By the time Margarita returned and sat down, the pap had been washed down the drain and the plate standing on the draining board. 'Churchie will be back soon,' she said brightly.

'So what's this about?' demanded Casca. She knew the game very well: first they pressed their useless gifts to indebt her, then they paraded their own needs. Well, Margarita would be disappointed this time. Casca folded her arms across her bosom and glared at the other woman, conscious that her facial muscles lacked the discipline to quell a brewing sneer.

In the days since Dr. Joda's bad news, Margarita had already chalked-up six snubs. She was rather used to cold shoulders. Before the age of 20, she wasn't dramatically different from many other girls in Keyside, except for her fairer complexion — and the fact that she had

Angelina for a mother. Her first daughter arrived at 20 and she had one son every year for the next five years. Her last daughter, Postie, was eight years old that year. If her life had a theme, it was: One Thing Led to Another. Or — considering the number of promises to marry she'd taken at face value — Believe This and You'll Believe Anything. Casca's impatient fingers crawled across the table in an angry tattoo. Margarita's hesitant hand settled on them and the room was silent but for the clock.

'You know of course,' began Margarita nervously, 'that I've given up my wayward ways.'

Casca had recoiled instinctively, pulling her hand away from her first human contact in months. It wasn't a reflection on who Margarita was, for Casca wasn't a warm person. Even her marriage had been primarily a business transaction. She wasn't a nasty person either, but the prospect of the imminent gossip on the poverty of her meals chafed at her wounded pride and gave a new cutting edge to what had never been a friendly tongue. 'Did you give them up, or did they give you up?'

Without warning, the muscles of Margarita's face began to jump spasmodically. Sympathy was another gift Casca didn't have, for she'd always felt personally in need of all the compassion she could dredge. Yet, she drew the line at cruelty. Despite being prepared for a beggar's practised tears, an almost tangible agony emanated from the crushed woman weeping under the weight of debts, Chief Banjo's notice to quit and Dr Joda's death sentence. It had never been a beautiful face. Now that it was contorting and streaming tears, Casca's most urgent instinct, as she put a hesitant hand on the trembling fist on her table, was the restoration of its tranquillity. When the tears ran dry, Margarita's hollowed eyes were red and frightened and a periodic sniff hinted at a potential Niagara in the wings. 'Can you believe I'm only 38?' she whispered. 'You must have heard I've got my mother's sickness.'

Casca stared. 'What is your mother's sickness?'

'The doctors had no name for it. I was 7 years old when she died.'

Casca remained silent. Instinct told her that further questions were dangerous, that a rapport was developing which would cause more heartache for the weeping woman when she tried to use it as a bridge for financial favours. Her hand slipped involuntarily from Margarita's.

'It isn't AIDS,' said Margarita without offence. 'I've passed that test. When my mother was deported from Italy, she was pregnant with me,' she ran her fingers through her hair, which wasn't quite Negroid and wasn't quite Caucasian. 'That's where I got this, you see. After she had me she never fully recovered. But I remember her headaches, — and the big boils in her armpits.' She pressed her fingers to her eyes, and, ever so slowly, raised her elbows until the angry red blisters in her armpits came into view. When her elbows returned to the table, Casca scolded severely.

'You had eighteen years to stop.'

'It was only last year that Jesus made sense to me,' Margarita replied. She lifted her head and sniffed. 'It was just because I couldn't say "No" to people. After all, what did I get out of it? Women hated and feared me, men used and dumped me...' She lifted her head another notch, and Casca saw that she was using gravity to keep fresh tears off her cheeks.

Casca had listened to too many lifetime rationalisations to be impressed. They all had their own stories. When they were twenty, they told it defiantly as they walked away with your husband's wallet. When they were fifty they told it tearfully as they walked away with your alms.

There was a minor clangour at the gate and seconds later, the young girl entered, bearing a large pumpkin. She was taller than both women, which still didn't make her particularly tall. Her hair and features were more African than her mother's. Her eyes had the regulation rebellion of the teenager, but Casca was mildly shocked to see something else there. She set the pumpkin on the table and turned awkwardly, with an unusual tenderness, towards her mother. 'Wait for me outside,' said Margarita firmly, her face averted. The girl hesitated and walked swiftly out.

'What's her name?' Casca asked, in spite of herself.

'Churchie.'

'Churchie?'

'I know what you're thinking. Churchill Mbanga isn't her father. Her full name is Churchyard. I named my children by the place of their conception.'

'How can you tell?'

Margarita's lips compressed suddenly, irritating Casca, who had never seen such sensitivity in a woman in her line of business.

'I'm not that kind of woman. I...'

Casca didn't know what type of woman she really was, and she didn't care. So far she was satisfied that she had missed nothing, all her weeks of hermitage. She rose. 'Tell me about it next time...'

'Dr Joda says I'm dying,' said Margarita with a quaking chin. 'He didn't say when, but he told me to cancel my damask outfit for the New Yam Festival... to save the money for my funeral feast.'

Casca sat down slowly. Keyside's New Yam festival was only a fortnight away. It dawned on her that Margarita's request might be more audacious than mere money. A single mother's concern at this point would obviously be fostering. Was it possible that she might actually want her to take on one of her bastards? But it was a request of such effrontery that Casca couldn't credit it, even to a one as impudent as Margarita. She took a deep breath and spent the last of her sympathy. 'I'm sorry,' she said.

'Don't sorry for me,' replied the retired entertainer bravely. 'It's the best thing for my daughter. Who was Neze before he married you? Yet, within six months his canteen was famous in Keyside. People keep calling you "miser, miser", and I keep asking them, "if you don't mise, where will the money for a house like this come from?" Your hands are good for making people...'

'Hey, hey,' said Casca sharply, cutting through the double-edged flattery. Her eyes flashed with that fire that kept the customers of Serene Canteen in their place through a decade of weaselling. 'What are we talking about here? Your mother and my husband's mother were second cousins. So? You must have closer relations in their dozens in Keyside — and even if you don't, Neze is dead.'

'I do have closer relations,' agreed Margarita, 'but Churchie doesn't. Neze was her father.'

There was a portentous silence in the room. Casca had never considered herself violent until that moment. Wild and raging thoughts flared from her mind like ranging bats hunting prey. The cleaver on the wall, the machete in the pail; all the innocuous implements of the expired moment suddenly became ominous instruments of death. 'Get out!' she whispered with the last of her self control, 'Take your bloody pumpkin and get out before I kill you!'

Margarita didn't stir. She was silent for a long minute then she shook her head. 'I've been preparing to die for weeks now,' she said quietly, 'but you can't kill the truth.'

'Truth!' snarled Casca, slamming her hands on the table with a force that knocked a flower vase onto its side. 'Truth from someone like you!' She rolled her eyes. 'A churchyard! Is anything sacred for you?'

'Women never accept!' sighed Margarita; 'This is not a reflection on you. Your husband was still a bachelor when Churchie was born. It was many, many years before he even met you...'

'Liar! Devil like you! We did many lab tests! Neze could never have fathered your child...'

'I don't care which lab told you so,' she patted her womb complacently. 'I trust my own equipment.'

'Neze kept no secrets from me.'

'He never knew,' replied Margarita. 'He was my cousin so there was no future in it. You're the first person to know Churchie's father — and you don't know how lucky you're to get her... I know her and I knew her father and let me tell you, only death could have taken this girl away from me...'

In her fury, Casca whirled around and hurled the stack of plates on the draining-board at Margarita, bringing the other woman involuntarily to her feet. The cascading china struck her before crashing on the table and shattering on the ground. Margarita clutched a numb elbow as she picked her way through broken pieces of china towards the door. An alarmed Churchie snatched away the door — and ducked as the pumpkin sailed through. The young girl stepped through and took her mother's arm. She gaped at Casca, more confused than angry. Margarita paused at the kitchen door and looked Casca in the face. She spat the tip of her tongue, a contemptuous gesture shorn of saliva. 'The villagers are right, you're a witch!' She turned and walked swiftly towards the gate, head held high. It was Casca's last sight of Margarita.

By Saturday when Ezeta brought his final instalment, the widow was still steaming from Margarita's provocation. Ezeta was at his most despondent. Despite the funds he had needlessly paid out, he was no closer to the title deeds of Serene Lodge. However, the Casca that met him at the gate knocked him off-balance. For the first time, the widow put away his money without counting it. — And she invited him into the house before he could steel himself to ask. She plied him with drinks and refrained from the subject of her interest until he was suitably garrulous.

Margarita's last words had jolted Casca out of the insularity of her depression. The longer she slept on them, the more obsessed she grew with her Keyside reputation, although she wouldn't have invested a kobo to improve it. Her hermitage project was in shreds. She was particularly consumed with the dread that Margarita's slanderous allegations concerning Neze and Churchie were now a matter of public gossip. But she was too embarrassed to ask Ezeta a direct question. The result was an unusually chatty Casca; which gave Ezeta a thoroughly wrong impression.

Emboldened by her hospitality, Ezeta upgraded his visits to a daily one. He found the widow's hospitality just as constant, but he had his own reasons to be cagey about local rumours, seeing no sense in spooking her with talk of her imminent death. She had therefore not made much progress on the matter of local gossip when Margarita died on schedule, six days after her visit to Serene Lodge.

Casca was stunned when her closet suitor conveyed the news, for he'd earlier assured her that Margarita had been sickly for decades. Margarita's death dampened the audacity of her desperate attempt to palm off her bastards onto wealthy villagers. Indeed, in Casca's eyes, that maternal instinct to provide for her children invested a dead Margarita with a nobility she didn't have in life. She immediately resolved to attend the wake and instructed Ezeta to escort her.

For Casca, it was also an opportunity to gauge the villagers' attitudes towards her; but a euphoric Ezeta put every possible wrong construction on his surprise date. Feeling that a 38-year-old woman's funeral would suitably underline the need for urgency in life, he scheduled his marriage proposal for their return from the wake. He made another new outfit, this time a sober lace caftan beaded with black and red tassels. He was so upbeat about his prospects that he noised his date abroad.

Unfortunately, his boasting inspired some undesired consequences. It was now thirteen weeks since Neze's death and Casca's robust health was a powerful indictment of those Keysiders who had enjoyed Neze's unstinting largesse. The occasion of her first public appearance since the murder and burial was a clear and logical opportunity to settle scores for Neze. By the evening of Margarita's wake, there were five separate full-blown conspiracies to do in Casca by means ranging from a surreptitious dagger to a sack furnished with a concrete slab and dispatched over the village quay.

The couple departed early for the wake, and Casca's punctuality defeated the first bumbling ambushers near Dr Joda's Hospital who regrouped and resolved to postpone their attack for her return journey. Margarita's wake was more modest than Neze's, but it wasn't less attended, for the news had spread that Casca was likely to attend — and unlikely to depart. There were no canopies or other excuses to spend money, but there was food aplenty.

Casca didn't get much honesty from Keysiders. Even the panting Ntume who slung his homicide team's bag of machetes on his back paused to shake her hand and inquire solicitously after her health. Casca studied Margarita's children as they sung away her soul, particularly the one she'd called Churchie. They were uniformly silent, uniformly sober, and uniformly handsome — and they looked too much like their mother to resemble any other Keysider.

The reverend spoke a long exhortation, taking his sermon from Jesus' teaching on the woman caught in adultery. Yet, his sermon completely missed its mark: if any woman in the gathering was in imminent danger of being stoned, it wasn't the one in the casket.

The exhortation ended. One or two helpers hauled the rostrum back to the churchyard next door. The covers were taken off the huge metal pots and Keysiders saw that the Margarita children were faithfully walking the plank of tradition into destitution. Churchie fended off whimpering mongrels as she started the chain that brought white disposable plates of pepper soup, rice and beef-stew flowing out to the mourners. Casca supposed she must go; she felt alien amongst Keysiders able to indulge unabashedly prodigious appetites in the presence of the orphans of a young, dead woman.

Which was just as well, for a squeamish vigilante squad had broken a vial of a bland rat poison into the plate of peppersoup before her. At that moment, the five youths privy to the poison plot were watching breathlessly, knowing that one sip would visiting a painful vengeance on the murderess. She ignored her plate and continued to watch the Margarita children as Ezeta ate the last of his peppersoup, blissfully unaware that the bag between his boot and Ntume's was bulging with instruments scheduled to hack his dreams of a wedding to death within the hour. One of the frustrated poison squad saw Ezeta's darting eyes and, anticipating his greed, bore Casca's uneaten peppersoup away not a moment too soon.

Chief Banjo arrived. The hopeful poisoners set a plate of rice and beef stew before Casca while she was distracted by his belated opening speech. Once again, she ignored her plate as Ezeta fell upon his meal; until, slowly, a peculiar change grew over her.

Before making the acquaintance of an apparition, it is impossible to predict one's reaction to ghosts. A look of terror flitted over Casca as she perceived a dead Neze. She leaned towards the food with dilated nostrils and grabbed Ezeta's arm. 'Who cooked this food?' she demanded.

'A very good cook,' mumbled Ezeta, through a mouthful of food.

Casca picked up the plate with trembling hands and bore it slowly to her nose, indifferent to the consternation she was provoking in watching Keysiders. She drank in the aroma of the food, her unseeing eyes passing over the surreptitious vigilantes. She swallowed. One nerveless hand reached for a spoon and no one was at all surprised when the plate slipped from the other and tipped over into a red mess on the sand. The poisoners were trembling in their shoes, unsure just how much Casca had deduced from her occultic study of the poisoned dish.

'Who cooked this?' Casca demanded from the serving lad as she took another plate from a roving tray.

'Churchie, of course,' came the response.

'Witchcraft!' she muttered, as she savoured the first spoon. Ezeta was already eating the bones on his plate. Underneath the table, two mongrels whined hungrily as they wolfed the spilled rice, their tails wagging anxiously at the prospect of interruption.

Night fell gradually.

The poison squad had fled. As the crazed dogs barked and convulsed to their death, they'd given up all hope of wresting retribution for Neze, convinced that Casca's spiritual powers of perception endangered fools who schemed against her. The other vigilante squads, ignorant of the fate of the first plot, began to mobilise themselves as the function ground to a close.

She supposed that the instruments of science would balk at her conclusions, but, like Margarita, it was a time for her to trust her own equipment. It seemed improbable that culinary serendipity, that ability to balance quantities of nutmeg and ginger to produce peculiar nuances of taste, could be so encoded in any concatenation of genes as to skip the broken link of nurture. Yet, she had the evidence of the stew. She wasn't a warm woman, and at 41 it was difficult for her to learn new ways. Yet, she was a woman of muscular convictions and she wrestled with the same single-minded, life-changing passions that seized her that evening, more than 10 years earlier, when she first ate Neze's stew.

The wake loitered towards an end, but no one departed. As the ambushers prepared to deploy themselves, only Ezeta and Casca were unaware that the high point of the wake was just around the corner. The widow felt the knocked engine of her natural drive aspirating again as a new, altruistic vision slowly overwhelmed her. She was no longer hungry, or fired by a life-and-death desperation; the fuel of her new drive was less basic, but far more combustible. Her new course was going to cost her; but she was already feeling alive for the expenditure — the very antithesis of depression. She took a deep breath and rose out of the rut the closure of Serene Canteen had swerved her into, realising too late, that one didn't share a bed with a man for ten years without becoming infected with whatever was ailing him.

The rumble of the wake disappeared into an unnatural silence as she approached the huddle that centred on the chief mourner. A ragged line of guests waited for their turn, pressing token notes into Churchie's hand while reserving their effusion for the sympathetic words they poured into the microphone. No one was particularly surprised to see Casca join the queue without a purse; still they strained to hear what she would say.

She took the microphone, her eyes fixed on Churchie who was clutching a teary Postie to her bosom. Casca blurted, with the abruptness of a person unused to public speaking: 'I sat down there, wondering what Neze would have done.' A long silence ensued, and it seemed Keysiders were also wondering. When Casca broke the silence, it seemed that something strange and frightening had overtaken the course of nature: it seemed as if a dog had just belched and apologised, as if Chief Banjo had just arrived early for a function, as if the embalmed Margarita had just sat up to taste an irresistible bean cake.

Casca began haltingly, 'I know you all think I'm a miser, but as somebody once said...' she paused as her memory failed her, then she bulldozed on, her voice losing its hesitancy as it hit the rancour of her natural tone, '... as I always say, the biggest misers are those with the deepest gullets and the most shallow pockets.' Then she took and held out Churchie's impoverished tray of crumpled notes and coins, glaring at those Keysiders bold enough to meet her gaze.

Gradually, the meaning of her words penetrated and another embarrassed queue of villagers built up in front of her, with a more generous round of donations. Thirty minutes later, as she carefully set down a tray from which currency notes were slithering, she had no way of knowing that she had just taken the biggest collection at any Keyside funeral. As Casca put away the microphone and turned to the disconsolate children, Keysiders watched the miserly widow narrowly, for she hadn't given a kobo herself. Her voice was scolding rather than sympathetic. 'Now don't be frivolous, you hear me? You mother had debts, so pay off every one of them. I don't want people pointing fingers at my foster children.'

In one sentence, she had already flabbergasted an entire village; but she was constitutionally incapable of the half-measure. The oldest of the boys had a stubborn dimple that remained on show, even when he was confused. 'What's your name?' Casca demanded of him.

'Palace,' he replied.

'Of all places!' she muttered to herself, nodding disapprovingly. Aloud, she asked: 'Do you drive?'

'Yes Ma'am.'

'When does that weasel want his house back?' Nobody had ever referred to Chief Banjo in such animalistic terms — at least in his presence; none of the children was bold enough to respond. 'Well tomorrow's just as good,' she concluded, 'Palace, once your mother is in the ground, come and take the family pick-up to fetch your things home.'

There were seven nods, which seemed to satisfy Casca. She began to turn away and then hesitated, as though she realised that the brevity and the public nature of the adoption may not have represented her character fairly to her new children. 'And let me tell you something about me,' she added more quietly, 'I don't take any nonsense.'

Then she turned and walked away. It was the signal for Ezeta to follow, but in the tumultuously insane onsets of the past half-hour, even he had recognised the futility of a marriage into the midst so many sturdy heirs. His engagement ring burned in his pocket as he reached for a passing bottle of beer, only just beating a hate-crazed Paddy to it.

A pent-up roar of conversation erupted as confused Keysiders reviewed the conventional wisdom on Casca. Slowly the certitude grew that if the widow had indeed killed Neze for his money, Keyside could do with a few more murderesses of her ilk. The disoriented vigilantes set down their bag of tricks and exchanged perplexed glances as their quarry made her lonely way home. They were like a murder jury on the threshold of a guilty verdict, who had just received a visit from the alleged deceased; for they had heard Casca for themselves; and the spirit of Neze was well.

Ψ

Has he quite finished now? grumbled an elderly mourner who had spent a much earlier decade waiting for Givemore to make a move.

Yes, Granny, shouted Dada into her better ear.

Then take me to the basin of akara! And stop whispering! That's how someone will waste one hour telling a story that nobody can hear.

*

Mother Clementina had arrived in the middle of Givemore's tale and was ushered to a seat near the graveside. She had come in with a strange woman who hung back at the fringes of the crowd, moving slowly from cluster to cluster. Ezinne had noticed her manoeuvres immediately, and knew she was no villager. When she passed close to Ezinne the school teacher's jaw had dropped at the sight of what she was wearing. Ezinne watched her narrowly thereafter, losing much of Givemore's story as she watched the newcomer's progress through Ma'Kanu's mourners. She was not particularly surprised to see her step over the bed of petunias, right into the inner circle that fringed the graveside, and work her way steadily until she was standing right behind Somto.

One more secret to share, saintly one, she muttered to herself.

Then Givemore fell silent and the woman leaned forward and murmured in Somto's ear: Is there truly a corpse in that blanket?

Somto whipped around. He almost fell into the grave in shock. Yyyyes. He said slowly. How did you get here?

You told me where you were born on the last page. She explained. She looked around. This has got to be the weirdest funeral I ever attended. — Counting our Mum's, where her creditors fought over the coffin *I* bought with my own money.

He took a deep breath and excused himself, hurrying forward in time to help Givemore up. He pulled up the stool, which had sunken several inches into the soft earth. That wasn't quite where the story ended. He whispered to the old man, Didn't you leave out the fire?

Givemore's smile was wan. I did, he agreed, But Churchie loved happy endings. His gnarled fingers gripped Somto. I have to go now, tradition forbids me to watch my junior go downstairs.

He made to go, but Somto's gentle voice detained him. You're her uncle Paddy, aren't you? He remained bowed over his stick for a while. When he finally looked up, his rheumy eyes had filled up.

It was unforgivable, what I did, but she forgave me. I was drunk and I was crazed with envy. She'd taken Postie to Dr Joda's hospital on the evening I burnt down Neze's house... Casca, Palace, all of them died. Only thing that kept me alive through prison was the thought that I might be able to make up to her and Postie, some-how... it was impossible, but *she forgave me*. She was a saint Somto... She was the real Saint... His voice broke.

Were you Neze's full-blood brother?

Same parents, he nodded.

What's your surname. Your *real* surname?

Nwazi, replied Givemore. With a huge effort, he squared his shoulders and Somto saw something in his deep eyes.

There's one more thing, Givemore,

What?

You have got to forgive yourself.

Givemore held the gaze for a few moments, then his shoulders slumped again and he turned wordlessly, picking his lonely way through the milling villagers.

Somto was rooted to the spot for several moments, marvelling at the ability of a sixty-year old crime to crush a very present life. As he stared down at Ma'Kanu's body, the name 'SomtoChukwu Nwazi' resonated in the stunned chambers of his mind. He bent down and touched her head, his fingers only just beating his tears. I *know* you, now, Ma. He whispered, Rest in peace.

Then he turned and made his way back to Coffey. When he was a few paces away, he decided that something about her was wrong. Something about her accoutrements clashed with the fish set jewel-lery she was wearing. Then he realised it was not *wrong* after all. She was only wearing an outsized male watch.

*

Mother Clementina was very cool about the absence of a coffin but the children of Orphan House were inflexible, so she stipulated a white blanket as a halfway house. They were in Grace Lodge, Njide and Ezinne, scavenging through the bundles of clothes in the attic, when Ezinne raised the subject. Those pictures, she began, avoiding Njide's eyes,

What pictures?

You know the pictures I mean, those two photographs of Udeme and Kanu that turned up between the pages of Ma's Bible. I find them very strange.

That makes two of us. Goes to show you. You think you know your own mum, and she dies and you find you never really *understood* her. Same thing with Somto and Tobe, you think you know your own brothers, then two short stories later, it turns out you didn't know jack ...

What I'm *actually* wondering, interrupted Ezinne impatiently, is whether I really understand my big sister: I didn't think you were so obsessed about happy endings for your tales...

Njide pulled a white blanket from a trunk and rose to her feet, sweating and flustered with the exertion. Here, she said, let's roll this out.

Ezinne took the roll off her sister, held one end, and tugged it firmly. It rolled out, a good length. It's long and white enough, she said shortly, About those photographs, one thing that strikes me as strange is...

Njide rolled the blanket up briskly. We've got to rush now dear, Ma'Kanu, Mother Clementina and the whole of Odozi are waiting. She straightened up and turned for Tobe's door. Just as she made the veranda, Ezinne caught her arm and brought her lips close to her ear. Those photographs, the orchid, did you *plant* them?

A scandalised Njide turned to stare at her sister. Ezi! she whispered. I'm *amazed* at you!

From the garden graveside where she and Kanu stood guard over Cecelia Wiggle, Udeme called impatiently, *Njide, come on!* She turned and hurried down the steps with the white blanket.

Ezinne reflected momentarily. She threw her head back and shouted, arms akimbo: That doesn't answer my question!

I'm *really* amazed at you! shouted back her sister, pushing her way through the mourners.

*

The last prayer had been said, the last word spoken. It hadn't been the simple internment Ma'Kanu envisaged, but as Odozi funerals went, it was quite simply, the briefest on record, lacking the ritual and ceremony that accompanied traditional burials. Kanu and Somto had lowered the body into the grave. Her bundle of keepsakes was laid by her side. Udeme set a bouquet of flowers at her head and her feet. The moment of emotion arrived and the children tossed in spadefuls of dirt and stepped back.

They managed to keep the tears away.

Mother Clementina sang a simple hymn as a token of farewell and commanded: Fill the grave, please.

Just then there was a cry from the villagers near the gate. Heads turned as Tobe pushed through the congested garden paths towards the graveside. When she saw him approach, Njide let out a victorious yell that clashed with the occasion, eliciting a frown from Mother Clementina. Ezinne was standing across the grave from Njide and their eyes met. Ezinne grinned and signed furtively: You didn't plan this one as well, did you?

The silent giant did not stop until he was standing by the grave beside Kanu. His face was as luminous as it was on the day he told Ma'Kanu the truth about his mother, Postie.

You're just in time, signed Njide, as Kanu passed him a spadeful of earth.

There was a sharp intake of breath from Tobe as he paused and looked into the grave. The frail form wrapped up in white contrasted sharply with the wet clods of red clay streaked with black. He let the scoop of earth fall in, stuck the spade into the red mound beside him and freed his hands to speak. I have something to say, he began.

Ezinne stepped higher on her mound of earth and projected her voice to carry across the garden. Listen up, everyone, Tobe has a final word for Ma'Kanu. The hubbub died down as the mourners quietened down to listen to the deaf mute.

It was the horror of the death sentence that struck me dumb, signed Tobe, I called a man 'Papa' and sentenced him to death... That was the great secret of my life, but two days ago, with Ma'Kanu, I lanced open that secret... like a boil...

He ran his hands over his head, waiting for Ezinne's translation. On her part, Ezinne faltered, she looked askance at her brother. Tobe's graveside oration was not starting at all typically. She turned her face away so he could not lip-read her translation: What it boils down to is this... Ma'Kanu was a mother with a difference... a mother with a difference...

After what seemed an age, Tobe raised his hands and continued: It was the horror of my patricide that struck me deaf. I couldn't bear to hear the screams of my dying father... But after thirty years I have confronted the horror. Two days ago, someone made me realise that none of it was my fault! Tobe clapped violently. He was smiling as he shook his head. He tapped his head as he continued: *I finally understood it up here!* The bondage was up here all the while, look at me! And brace yourselves for the truth!

Ma'Kanu was a wonderful woman... a really, *really* wonderful woman..., translated an agitated Ezinne, she met Njide's eyes and shook her head ever so slightly. It was the signal to rein in their intense brother. It was good to see Tobe at the funeral, but a graveside oration was not quite the forum to confess his role in a thirty-year-old patricide. Njide caught on quickly and edged towards Tobe.

She never made it.

Tobe put his hands in his pockets, cleared his throat, and vocalised: Ezinne, thanks, but I think I'd better speak for myself from now on! The voice was gruff and rusty, running words together and mauling consonants. It was clearly not yet ready for a public outing, and the sounds themselves could only be called 'words' by an act of charity — but all the same, they provoked a roar of consternation from the villagers of Odozi who had grown up with the inarticulate Tobe.

Ezinne whirled around seeking the source of the voice, disbelieving the evidence of her eyes and ears. The keenest screams came from Udeme and Njide who were caught up by several hands. Isolated on her mound, the speechless Ezinne was not so fortunate. When she lost the strength in her legs, she buckled into the grave in a faint to incommode her long-suffering mother one final time.

<End>

Short Story Anthology.
Published, 1.1.12
PB ISBN: 978-978-2190-10-9
309pp
140mm x 214mm

"A feast of words awaits any reader who picks up The Ghost of Sani Abacha...No two stories are alike...These stories are told in a deeply humorous way that makes you laugh all through the book, even as you reflect on the fate of the people who fill each page – people who become more real to you because of their flaws. They are so alive you half-expect them to jump out of the pages..." – A. Olofintuade in Daily Times.

The Ghost of Sani Abacha is a humorous collection of incisively observed short stories set in a post-autocratic country whose indigenes have varying levels of PTSDs (Post Traumatic Stress Disorders) from three decades of military occupation. In the title story, a fledgling politician walks a tightrope between a conscience and the inspiration of dictator Sani Abacha's lifestyle, determined to avoid his mentor's colourful death in the laps of imported prostitutes.

In *Gluttony*, a hungry village has one day to eat a beached whale before it rots in a humorous retelling of the Biblical account of Jonah and the whale… In the pages of this writer's fiction, the revolutionaries are inarticulate (*Bullfight*), the lovers are cowed - with husbands recruiting wives to brothels (*A Roman Job Offer*). The characters are as impishly devious as their circumstances are desperate (*The Las' Foolscap, Confessions of the General's Marabout, A History of Human Servitude*). This is a major collection of 26 stories (including 17 appearing for the first time) from a master ironist, in the author's first fiction book in 7 years.

Novel.
Ist Published: 2003
Gwandustan Edition: 2013
PB ISBN: 978-978-2190-13-0
193pp
140mm x 220mm

"An incredibly comical book but full of tragic unnuendoes – I find myself laughing aloud even as I reflect on the dark fate of the characters. The book seems to affect me emotionally. I don't know why. I am usually immune from such cathartic effects" – Jahman Anikulapo, former editor, Guardian on Sunday.

Diaries of a Dead African explores its life-threatening themes with native humour. Meme Jumai and his two sons – Abel (failed writer) and Calamatus (aspiring conman) – document the final days of their desperate struggle to retain the vanishing shreds of their dignity.

At last, Abel's fondest dreams were coming true. Yet, his father had died at 50 and his brother at 25. How to outlive them both – without fleeing the very opportunities he had craved all his life...

Meme's Diary was first published in *London Review of Books* in 2001, and has been translated into Italian in *La Internazionale*. The book was first published in 2003, and the sharp contrast between the startling comedy of the narration and the tense cicumstances of the diarists is as fresh as ever in this 10th anniversary edition of a new humour classic.

Short Story Anthology
Published Nov, 20th 2013
PB ISBN:
978-978-2190-15-4
290 pp   117mm x 180mm

"Nwokolo's stories are outstanding in seamlessly combining exterior, social worlds with interior reflection. He effortlessly explores the minutiae of social exchanges, misunderstanding and embarrassment, but always manages to add in a multiplier – so that from these small moments he can shine a light on broader social themes" Emma Anderson, Manchester Art Gallery

During his own wake keeping, Ali is lucky enough to recover from his coma, but his cheap casket and disgraceful grave clothes cause matrimonial problems [*The Resurrection of Djema Ali*]…

Following his well-received 2012 short story collection [The Ghost of Sani Abacha], Chuma Nwokolo delivers another major anthology, *How to Spell Naija in 100 Short Stories,* in time for the 100th year of Nigeria's unification in 2014. The stories in this first volume of 50 tales have the author's trademark humour and insight. The strong presence of flash fiction (about half the stories are less than 1,000 words in length) makes this collection both accessible and readable. These fifty tales take the reader from the domestic to the political and from village into Diaspora. The private circumstances of politicians, housewives, kidnapers and ram-sellers come to life as each plot unfolds themes that range from forgiveness to social media, from food to seduction.

The next volume of 50 tales is due in 2014.

Poetry Anthology
Published 1st June, 2014.
PB ISBN:
978-978-2190-16-1
HB ISBN:
978-978-2190-18-5

"I will
tell you how
big a deal I am, he said:

the god
you worship
brings his tithes to Me"

– Neo-Colonial Njakiri

The hundred poems in this anthology strike a balance between orthodoxy and rebellion, between modern and heritage. The poetic voice is poised between the caustic and the comic, but the lines are always insightful. With Nigeria for foreground, the poems veer from the old Sudan to the new South Africa, from science to terrorism, exploring themes from war to weddings and always provoking the reader to a second, more surprised look at the lived life even as trees, rivers, planets - and of course, minor gods - find their peculiar voice.

This is Nwokolo's first poetry collection in the eight years since *Memories of Stone* [2006].

www.ingramcontent.com/pod-product-compliance
Lightning Source LLC
Chambersburg PA
CBHW051430130726
47987CB00005B/1985